D0312273

"I LOVE this book. Mira Kirshenbaum has provided an incredible tool for today's time-starved couples: an easy-to-follow, sensible approach to reconnecting. *The Weekend Marriage* helps you quickly get to the important issues that make or break your relationship, and shows you how to fast-forward through all the time-wasting interactions that can derail you. My husband and I couldn't believe how well—and quickly—this practical approach works to help you rediscover a great connection! I want twenty copies to send to everyone I know, because every couple I know needs this book."

> —**Mary Shomon,** patient advocate and author of
> *Living Well with Hypothyroidism, the Thyroid Diet*

"As a psychologist and a husband, I found Mira Kirshenbaum's new book, *The Weekend Marriage,* to be wonderfully practical and helpful for real-life marriages. I'll use her insights personally and professionally!"

> —**Ross Porter, Ph.D.,** clinical psychologist and author
> of *To Kindle a Fire*

"Mira Kirshenbaum's books are always a breath of fresh air. Clear, simple, and light hearted, *The Weekend Marriage* evokes hope and teaches the how-to's of making a marriage work. Kirshenbaum reminds us how *not* to let it slip away, how to hold it and enfold it into our daily lives so that marriages grow and thrive, even in a time-starved world."

> —**Dr. Dorothy Firman,** psychotherapist and author of
> *Daughters and Mothers: Making It Work* and *Chicken
> Soup for the Mother and Daughter Soul*

"Mira Kirshenbaum has once again provided readers with strategies to cope with one of America's major problems. Our marriages are suffering from the fast pace of our lives and the inordinate pressures we all face. Kirshenbaum gives readers ways to remain balanced with the ones we cherish. Read this book, practice the insights provided, and pass it on to all those who want to preserve intimacy in these troubled times."

> —**Arthur P. Ciaramicoli, Ed.D., Ph.D.**, author of
> *Performance Addiction: The Dangerous New Syndrome
> and How to Stop It from Ruining Your Life*

"*The Weekend Marriage* offers simple yet magical solutions to the everyday life of couples with limited time together. Husbands and wives who struggle with keeping the flame burning will find fresh and practical advice to rejuvenate the lifeblood of their unions. Readers will learn how to relinquish negative habits that pull spouses apart and learn instead to heighten love and romance in marriage."

> —**Eva Fogelman, Ph.D.**, psychologist and author
> of *Conscience and Courage: Rescuers of Jews During
> the Holocaust*

ALSO BY MIRA KIRSHENBAUM

Everything Happens for a Reason:
Finding the True Meaning of the Events in Our Lives

The Emotional Energy Factor:
The Secrets High-Energy People Use to Beat Emotional Fatigue

Too Good to Leave, Too Bad to Stay:
A Step-By-Step Guide to Helping You Decide
Whether to Stay In or Get Out of Your Relationship

The Gift of a Year:
How to Give Yourself the Most Meaningful,
Pleasurable, and Satisfying Year of Your Life

Women & Love:
The Eight Make-or-Break Experiences of Love in Women's Lives

Our Love Is Too Good to Feel So Bad:
The 10 Prescriptions to Heal Your Relationship

Parent/Teen Breakthrough:
The Relationship Approach (with Dr. Charles Foster)

THE WEEKEND MARRIAGE

Abundant Love in a Time-Starved World

MIRA KIRSHENBAUM

Harmony Books / New York

Published in the United States by Harmony Books,
an imprint of the Crown Publishing Group,
a division of Random House, Inc., New York.

www.crownpublishing.com

Harmony Books is a registered trademark and the Harmony Books
colophon is a trademark of Random House, Inc.

Library of Congress Cataloging-in-Publication Data
Kirshenbaum, Mira.
The weekend marriage : abundant love in a time-starved world / Mira
Kirshenbaum. — 1st ed.
1. Marriage. I. Title.
HQ734.K53 2005
646.7'8—dc22   2004021734

ISBN 1-4000-8098-3

Printed in the United States of America

Design by Chris Welch

10 9 8 7 6 5 4 3 2 1

First Edition

TO CHARLES

ACKNOWLEDGMENTS

No one has all the answers, but almost everyone has some answers. These are the people who deserve my first and most heartfelt thanks: the men and women who were so patient, so eager to help when I asked them, "What do you do to have a good relationship given the fact that you don't have much time for each other?" But beyond great answers to this question they gave me another gift. They talked about how they hadn't always had these answers. It took trial and error. So besides the gift of help they have given the gift of hope. I'm deeply grateful.

It's a joy to me to acknowledge the part my husband, Dr. Charles Foster, played in writing this book. The fact is, *The Weekend Marriage* is just as much his book as it is mine. We were full partners in researching and writing it. Every word here is as much his as it is mine. Oh, and by the way: thanks for being a great husband too!

I have a lot of people to thank at Harmony Books, that

wonderful hive of light. First and foremost there's my brilliant editor Kim Meisner. What a pleasure it's been to work with her. She's put her heart and soul into this book. To do such an excellent job of putting up with me, getting what I'm trying to say, and then bringing that out is very special.

Without Shaye Areheart, my friend, mentor, and all-around good genie, this book would not have happened. Words of thanks fail me.

Selina Cicogna, my gifted publicist, does such a great job, cares so much, and manages to be so sweet to me. It means so much. Thanks also to the other terrific publicity people, and to Kira Stevens, Jill Flaxman, and Tara Gilbride.

Thanks to Julie Will for being so smart and helpful, and for being such a pleasure to work with.

Howard Morhaim, my agent, is quite simply the best. He takes such good care of me. He's so smart. He's such a good person. What more could you ask for?

We all have a kitchen cabinet we turn to for advice and support. I'm so grateful that the two most important members of my kitchen cabinet are my loving daughters, Rachel and Hannah. Who could've known, when they were little, that they'd grow up to be so wise?

CONTENTS

THE
WEEKEND
MARRIAGE

Chapter One

WHAT IS THE WEEKEND MARRIAGE?

I t took years before it finally hit me: *Oh my God, I don't have time for my marriage!* How could I have missed it? After all, I knew that it's hard to have a relationship if you don't have time for it. Time is the air love needs to breathe. But when you're suffocating slowly, it can take a long while to realize what's really going on.

It's not that I'd been working every minute. But I saw that the pace of my life, plus my husband's busy life, meant we were too often like ships passing in the night. No, change that. Like two New York City taxis that every now and then find themselves waiting at the same red light together.

This is *the weekend marriage*. It's the marriage most of us have these days: during a typical week you have only minutes, not hours, to spend feeling like a couple—getting close, having fun together, feeling intimate. It's *not* one of those rare situations where one person works in a far-off city Monday through Friday. In the weekend marriage you and your spouse sleep under the same roof most nights but you rarely have enough time for each other except on weekends. If then.

Few of us are exempt. Whoever is busiest or most drained determines how much time the two of you have together. If he or she has only a few minutes a day for the relationship, that's all the relationship gets.

When I saw what was happening in my marriage, it scared me, as it does so many of us. I knew in my bones that neglect is how you kill a relationship, just the way neglect kills pets, plants, and other vulnerable living things. And we're right to be scared. I've learned that the weekend marriage is now the most important and least understood reason why couples end up getting divorced.

Like many of us, I felt guilty. What kind of person was I to make my relationship such a low priority?

But I also felt angry. With my husband first of all. Didn't he care enough to call us back from the mad pace of our lives? But the thing is, he had. We both had. "We need to get away," we'd say. "We need to spend more time together." But we didn't do much about it—we were too busy to make plans! Then, stupidly enough, I was angry with life. It didn't seem fair that there's no time left for love if you live the way you're supposed to—work hard, keep up your home, spend time with family, and do all the other things that come along with being responsible and living a normal life.

But it wasn't *just* about not having time for each other. I noticed that something weird happens when you go from having plenty of time together, like when you're first starting out, to not having much time. You'd think that the good and bad ways you used to interact would shrink in the same proportions. You'd spend less time making love and having nice easy conversations, but you'd also spend less time arguing and being mad at each other.

But the proportions don't stay the same. The bad stuff—the disagreements, the irritability, the misunderstandings—seem to take up more time than they did before. It's the good stuff that gets squeezed out. Here's Kirshenbaum's Variation on Murphy's Law: the less time you have together, the more things go wrong in your relationship.

No wonder a lot of marriages are ending these days that should survive. Couples are battling forces that are too much for them: too much stress and not enough time. If this pattern of life continues, the divorce rate will only climb. And a rising divorce rate will discourage people from entering into committed relationships.

Something must be done about this. But what?

It would be great if we could get together as a society and fix this. We desperately need to live in a more family-friendly environment, which would give people more time for their relationships. If we made a national commitment to do this, I'm convinced the divorce rate could be cut by more than half. But there's nothing on the horizon that shows we're even close to making a commitment to becoming a more family-friendly society. On the contrary, global economic forces are pushing people in the countries we compete with to work harder. In that environment, how can we work less?

So that leaves us needing to find solutions as individuals. And here I bring good news. I know from direct experience that people *can* learn to protect their relationships from the ravages of the time crunch, and if they do, that too would cut the divorce rate enormously.

I believe in marriage, and what's more I believe most marriages today can be far better than people imagine. The fact that we're dealing with a new reality is a tremendous opportunity. But we need some coaching.

Think of how the two of you are dealing with each other these days. Is it working for you? Probably not. It's time to try something else. We can't keep ignoring the impact of our lives on our love. We can't pretend anymore that lack of time doesn't make a difference. We can't keep putting off all the healing we know our relationships need for that time "one day" when time is no longer a problem. The lives we lead today are a recipe for loneliness, for bitterness, for feeling guilty that we're not able to make things better, for fear of where the distance and anger are bringing us.

This is where so many divorces come from. I'm not talking about the divorces that come when people realize what a stupid choice of partner they've made. No, I'm talking about the sadder, more common divorces that leave people asking each other, "Where did our love go?" There was once real love, but it got chewed up in the time crunch.

Until now we haven't understood how the lives we lead damage love, and we haven't known what to do about it. How do you solve problems that come up between you if there's no time to talk? How do you deal with anger if there's no time to heal the hurts? How do you make good things happen and rebuild your relationship if you're always using the little time you have to put out fires? How do you balance your needs and your partner's?

I had these questions, too. So I started doing research. I figured that there had to be couples out there who would prove that we don't have to be starved of love just because our lives are starved of time. It took me years, but I found their secrets.

I now know that you and I can thrive even in the midst of a time-starved lifestyle.

And that's where this book comes in. It provides the insights and tools you need to protect your love and keep it strong. That's why I wrote it. Until we change the way we live as a society, we're going to have to protect our stressed and harried marriages one relationship at a time.

In this book you'll see how to deal with the real issues between you and your partner *and* make sure your needs get met *and* recapture the joy, intimacy, and abundant love you've been longing for. I'll tell you one thing: it turns out to be a lot easier to do it right than to do it wrong.

THE PROBLEM

Chapter Two

LIVING THE
WEEKEND MARRIAGE

Once upon a time there were a prince and a princess.

The prince's name was Bill. Of course he wasn't a real prince. But his buddies thought he was a prince of a guy. And he had some of the dreams real princes have, like the dream of one day finding his own princess and living happily ever after with her.

The princess's name was Laura. She wasn't a real princess, either. But she looked a bit like a princess, especially on her good days, and some of the guys she'd gone out with thought she was worthy of being a princess. Although she didn't put on airs, sometimes she wanted to be treated a little like a princess. She also had some of the dreams princesses have, like the dream of one day finding her own prince and living happily ever after.

And one day Prince Bill and Princess Laura found each other, just like in a fairy tale, just as if destiny had intended it. After many adventures, where a couple of times they thought they might lose each other, they got married. They had every hope of living happily ever after.

As they rode off into the sunset together, what they looked forward to most was a life filled with love. Not just love as a fact, something that you know is there the way you know you have a marriage certificate buried somewhere among your papers. Bill and Laura wanted to hold on to what they had—a love that's alive, that they experience every day.

When love is alive, Laura said (and Bill agreed), there's real affection. There's hand-holding, hugs, and kisses. There are long, sweet conversations that connect the two of you and make you feel good about each other. There's having the kind of fun together that makes you feel you're special. There's sitting opposite each other at a small table in a quiet restaurant, talking, laughing, looking into each other's eyes. There's going for long walks together where you're perfectly happy saying nothing. There's lying in bed contentedly in each other's arms. There's making love when you have enough time so it's more than just something you're fitting in.

But once our prince and princess started trying to live happily ever after, something terrible happened. A dark and evil monster appeared in their lives. This monster could lurk invisible for days, but then it would pop up and try to drag them down into a black pit of misery. Occasionally Bill and Laura got away from it. But in a little while the monster would get them again. They could never catch their breath.

What's this monster I'm talking about?

The monster is not the weekend marriage itself. Some couples have figured out how to do well in spite of their time-starved lifestyle. No, the monster is the way most of us let the weekend marriage affect us. Watch. . . .

IT'S FIRST THING Monday morning. Bill and Laura's clock radio comes on and suddenly it's like the beginning of a mad race. There's no time to lie under the covers and slowly wake up snuggled together. Instead, Bill jumps out of bed and heads off to the kitchen to get the coffee going. Laura groggily stumbles into the shower.

Here's what happens in that crazy hour after Bill and Laura wake up. Their two kids are dragged complaining out of bed and stuffed into clothes. Breakfasts get thrown together and sandwiches tossed into lunch boxes. Bill constantly barks questions and commands at Laura, but she can only wonder to herself yet again, *Why can't I have a quiet, peaceful morning where no one bugs me? I'm not even awake yet.* They gulp down their coffee in whatever spare seconds they can find. And Laura once again munches her toast standing over the kitchen sink to save the time it would take to rinse a plate.

Bill and Laura happen to have kids. But the monster also stalks couples without kids. They, too, lead stressed-out, time-deprived lives. I understand: kids take up a ton of time. I have two kids myself. But couples without kids often pile on extra responsibilities at work. They're often developing artistic or business sidelines. Perhaps they're taking courses. They often have large social networks. And there goes their free time. So we're all pretty much in the same boat.

And the monster's just as busy stalking couples where only one of you works outside the home. Laura goes out to work every day, but even if she were busy at home, whoever worked hardest or longest would determine how much leftover time they'd have together.

Bill and Laura can't remember the last morning during the week that they were able to sit down and chat over a leisurely breakfast or even share a peaceful ten minutes together over a cup of coffee. The one thing Bill and Laura hear from each other more than anything else in the morning is *Stay out of my way— I'm running late.*

During the day, Bill and Laura work at a faster pace than people have at any time in human history. You just can't get the job done anymore unless you multitask. At the same time, they're in frequent cell-phone or e-mail contact with each other. But they're not exchanging love talk. Their chatter is about irksome family details, like who's going to stop by the dry cleaners, who's going to pick up which kid when, who's going to call the plumber, who's going to handle the latest crisis in their whack-a-mole lives.

When they eventually get home, it's late. They're hungry, but there's not much time to make a meal. They can't remember the last time they cooked a real dinner on a weekday. These days dinner is more often thrown together or ordered in than slow cooked. Tonight, Bill and Laura's dinner comes from the local pizza place. They have gourmet dreams but they lead fast-food lives.

They also arrive home stressed to the max. Every demand someone made of them during the day, every question someone asked, every glitch they ran into—all this was like water dropping onto a sponge that started the day dry. What's a drop of water here and there? But the sponge can absorb only so much, and by now Bill and Laura have had it. They can't absorb another drop of stress.

But they have different needs when they get home. Laura would love nothing more than to zip through the many chores they still have to do so they can have some free time later on. But this is the time of day when Bill's in an energy slump. The first thing he needs is some peace and quiet.

Their different needs mean there's tension in the air by the time Bill and Laura have cleaned up the kitchen, helped the kids with homework, put them to bed, fed the cat, walked the dog, paid some bills, made a couple of calls for work, and checked their e-mail. Now it's late. All they both want to do is collapse in front of the TV. It seems TV was invented to fill the time when you're too tired to do anything but it's too early to go to sleep.

And that was just Monday. It's like that every weekday, except that Laura has to work late on Tuesday, there's a parents' night at school on Wednesday, and Thursday evening Bill has to run over to his sister's house. She's a single mom and he has to help her fix her sink.

What's it like for Laura and Bill to have a relationship in the midst of all this? It's not a stroll on the beach at sunset, I can tell you that. But I don't have to tell you that, because you know it already. You live it.

But everyone lives it a little differently. At one point Bill said, "I'll tell you what it's like for me. I get home, we have a quick kiss hello, we each give the other the thirty-second summary of our day, and then we mostly talk about problems. It's all 'Did you remember to . . . ?' 'Did you get a chance to call . . . ?' 'We've got to do something about . . .' 'When do you plan to . . . ?' 'Have you thought anymore about . . . ?' 'Why didn't you . . . ?' 'Why won't you . . . ?' 'Why can't you . . . ?' *Where's the love in all this?*"

Laura's take was a little different: "I'm just as tired as you are in the evening. But you just want to collapse in front of the TV. I'd love to do that but there's so much stuff we have to deal with and someone's got to take care of things around here. How do you think I feel being put in the position of worrying about all this stuff? It's just not fair."

Like most of us, Bill and Laura know there's something wrong with their harried lives. This is not what *happily ever after* was supposed to be. They still love each other, of course. They're pretty sure they're *in* love. But, they both think, *We used to be such a great couple. Even if it wasn't perfect, we did fun things together and we were so into each other. We got along so well. What happened to us? I can't find myself in our lives and I can't find the couple we used to be.*

It's a mistake to think that sophisticated people who've spent their lives talking about relationship problems can talk their way out of the time crunch. No matter how smart you are, you get caught up in the same vicious cycle. The less time you have together, the more problems creep in. The more problems you have, the more you talk about them. The more you talk about them, the more your relationship is dominated by "problem talk," and the less you want to spend time together. No wonder the most common problem couples have is not being able to get close, not feeling connected.

But under the pressure of a time-starved lifestyle, everything Bill and Laura have learned about working on their relationship soon becomes useless. It's like someone who's great at cooking for friends when he has all the time in the world and no pressure—put him in a restaurant kitchen during Friday evening rush and he could easily be reduced to a quivering mass of jelly.

BUT WAIT A minute. Aren't Saturday and Sunday supposed to come riding to the rescue, offering gifts of time and rest? In theory, yes. But in reality, it's not much better. On Saturday, Bill and Laura have to wake up early and get the kids ready to drive out to visit her parents. They come home late Saturday and they're tired again. Sunday morning one of the kids has soccer. Sunday afternoon they're out shopping.

You might ask, doesn't family time count toward relationship time, like when Bill and Laura spent the day with their kids and her parents, or when they go shopping or do chores together?

Hey, nothing's better than good family time. But family time doesn't bring a couple close in that warm, sexy, romantic, intimate way we all need. Just ask empty nesters or divorced couples who poured their hearts into creating good family time but then found that there was little left between them. Why? Because they'd done very little that counted as real love time. Couples have an absolute need to spend time together the way they did when they were first in love. This is the only kind of time that keeps love alive, and it's the first casualty of the weekend marriage.

Of course Bill and Laura do manage to spend some time together on the weekend. Too often, unfortunately, it's tainted. Swept up by the pace and pressure of their week, there were many instances where they'd stepped on each other's toes, where there'd been a flare-up of anger, where they'd hit an air pocket of disappointment. At every turn, patience was at a premium. Their frustration didn't always show itself in anger. Sometimes it got expressed by silence—they'd seem polite, but inside each felt sad and cold.

And there were constant missed opportunities for small acts of affection or closeness—the hand that wasn't taken, the kiss that was broken off too soon, the word of support that wasn't spoken. When you're this far apart, it can take a long time to find your way back to warmth and intimacy.

That Sunday evening, by some kind of miracle, the kids are tired enough to go to bed early. Bill and Laura suddenly find themselves with three hours all their own. But there is a burden of annoyance to clear through first.

Laura doesn't feel they can slow dance in the living room to their favorite music until they deal with how hurt she was by the way last Tuesday Bill cavalierly dismissed her worries about the kids as if she were a ninny. Bill is still fuming because Laura didn't get the papers to the bank on time for their mortgage refinance application. And they still have to have a long conversation about whether it's time to get a new car, and that would bring up all kinds of money issues that are no fun to deal with.

So there's no slow dancing. There's no slow talking, either—those long, leisurely conversations where Bill and Laura would talk about everything and nothing the way they did when they were first in love. Instead there's talking about problems. It's not much fun talking about problems to begin with, but the sense of time pressure they feel just makes things worse.

They finally make up, though. And sometime late Sunday night they manage to make love. But Bill and Laura both admitted that it wasn't because they got to the point of feeling all that sexy or intimate. It was just that they didn't want another week to go by without having sex.

Later, they lie in bed side by side, trying to fall asleep, feeling a little sad and disconnected from each other, as if a wonderful opportunity had been lost.

THE THING IS that if they'd really speak the truth of their hearts, they'd see that they are in total agreement: *It's bad enough that we're having trouble getting along,* they each would say, *but what really caps it off is this sense that I've tried everything and now I don't know what to do. I try to hold my tongue; then I insist that we talk until we're exhausted. I try to be as generous as I can be; then I think maybe it would be better if I focused on my own needs. I overlook things; then I struggle over stupid little things. But I'm really trying. It just doesn't make sense that this adds up to a marriage filled with problems.*

Bill and Laura aren't alone. The details may vary, but millions of us share in their hopes and struggles and confusion.

But wait a minute, you might say. *Can it really be true that most of our relationship problems come from our not having much time together?*

Well, you tell me. . . .

Chapter Three

THE NO-TIME-FOR-LOVE TEST

T he truth is that no one has time to be in a relationship anymore. Americans are now the rushing-around-est people in the history of the world. We work more hours per day and spend more days per year on the job than people in any other developed country.

Of course we do our best to cope with all this pressure. We multitask, even though the stress of it hurts us. We eat fast food, although we know that eating nothing but fast food can kill you. We sacrifice this, juggle that, and still there's never enough time.

"But," you might say, "I know I'm busy, but how do I know that it's the weekend marriage that's making things hard in my relationship? Isn't there such a thing as people just not getting along?"

A good way to determine if it's your time-starved lifestyle that's been causing the problems in your relationship is to take the no-time-for-love test:

Think about the last few times you and your spouse spent a good chunk of free time together *just the two of you*. It could be when you went on a relaxing vacation. Or when you got away for a whole weekend. Or even when you found a few hours to go out for a long romantic dinner. Does it usually feel better to be together when you have this extended couple time? Or does it feel worse?

This no-time-for-love test, developed in the course of my research, accurately determines whether your problems come mostly from the fact that you have no time for love or mostly from how you fit together as individuals.

Naturally, this test asks about your *general* pattern. After all, anything can happen any one time. The happiest couple in the world might start off on the wrong foot and end up being mad at each other throughout a three-day vacation. And couples very often need to spend a little time getting back in sync if they've been mad at each other.

But if things have generally felt better between you when you managed to spend some quality time together just the two of you (no children, no friends, no family), then your relationship has been suffering from a time problem, not a people problem or a fit problem. You're victims of the weekend marriage.

This test makes sense. If a couple's relationship gets *worse* when they go on vacation, the problems are caused by who they are—because, for example, one finds the other boring or mean or irresponsible or overcritical—or because they're just not compatible. People take their problems with them wherever they go, don't they? If there's a fundamental problem with the relationship itself, then the more time people have together, the more opportunities there are for their problems to come out of the woodwork. The weekend marriage was actually saving these people from seeing how poorly they got along.

But what if your relationship usually gets *better* when you spend time together?

Maybe there was a time a couple of weeks ago when you both woke up early Saturday morning, made some coffee, and had a couple of hours together just hanging out in bed. Remember how you laughed? And how you talked about things you hadn't talked about in a long time?

Maybe there was a three-day weekend where the kids were off with their grandparents. Okay, you were busy most of Saturday, but you had a wonderful Sunday together. And most of Monday. And you were surprised at how much you enjoyed each other, how comfortable you felt together.

In cases like these, it has to be the changed environment that made the difference. Who you are as people didn't change. What changed was your suddenly having relaxed, free time for each other. Mystery solved. You're a weekend-marriage couple: whenever you slip out of the grip of the time crunch, you return to being the loving, fun couple you used to be together and who deep down you believe you still are.

It's time we paid attention to the effects of our time-starved lifestyle on marriage. Talk about relationships has been dominated for too long by talk about the differences between the sexes. I think we're tired of pinning *all* our problems on male/female differences. Come on—is that really our biggest challenge? So enough already. The sexes are different, but they've been different forever. What has changed is that now people don't have enough time for each other.

We can't keep putting off the healing we know our relation-ship needs for that time "one day" when time is no longer a problem. But if you passed the no-time-for-love test, that healing can start now.

The test proves that the monster attacking your relationship is a paper tiger. When you gave yourselves a real chunk of time to-gether, the monster couldn't prevail. The crap that had built up between you began to melt away.

If you're a weekend-marriage couple, it really does feel as though you are being stalked by an invisible monster, doesn't it? And the worst part is how it makes you think that your spouse is the monster, and it makes your spouse think that you're the mon-ster. And then it watches you turn on each other, and it laughs.

This is the monster in action. It's spawned by the trouble we have trying to love each other while we're living the weekend marriage. We've been blaming each other and ourselves for our problems for too long.

Of course sometimes blame feels so right. *It's because my spouse is a jerk, a nag, a bore, a bitch, a thug, a nut, a big fat baby . . .*—fill in your own label. But blame obviously hasn't helped us. It hasn't clarified anything. If you don't grasp the fact that the weekend marriage is what's to blame for most of your problems as a cou-ple, you'll never be able to figure out why things are going wrong between you and what to do about it.

Sometimes we play the blame game in a more sophisticated way. We say there are problems because "we have trouble com-municating" or "because we're just too different." This leads to solutions that focus on improving communication or bridging differences, as if that would get to the root of what's wrong. But would that solve your problems?

Well, it's certainly true that people sometimes find they have trouble communicating. And it's very easy for two people to feel like alien creatures to each other. But let's take a second look at whether it makes sense that these really are the underlying reasons for all the difficulties we see out there in weekend-marriage couples.

Two people fall in love and get married. They had to have something going for them that enabled them to get through all the hurdles from the first date to their wedding day. After all, of all the people who go on a first date with each other, how many end up getting married? *Less than 2 percent.* The couples who survive this rigorous weeding-out process generally feel they got as far as they did because they were communicating so well and because they felt they meshed together in so many ways.

The overwhelming majority of couples who end up in trouble started out doing just fine. Any attempt to understand what happens to marriages has to deal with this basic fact. Something happens to cause problems in an otherwise strong, healthy relationship. And that "something" is probably not the people themselves, because we know that there was a period when they were doing fine.

Let's not kid ourselves: if you're married to someone who's no good, or who's no good for you, *get the hell out of the marriage.* It may take time to see the truth, but you have only one life and you shouldn't spend a minute of it stuck with the wrong person.

Most of the time, though, this doesn't apply. You *are* married to the right person. You knew what you were doing when you fell in love and got married. I don't want to oversimplify, but if you're like most of us, you dragged your poor old imperfect self into a commitment with your spouse's poor old imperfect self. And you did so because there was a lot of good stuff there in spite of the imperfections. I'm *sure* that's why you got married. It's why almost *everyone* gets married. Not because you don't think that there's any bad stuff. But because you believe in the good stuff—like a warm smile, a good sense of humor, a deep streak of honesty and loyalty and kindness, a healthy dose of common sense, some sexual chemistry, and a couple of interests you share. It's things like this that make it all worthwhile and that enter into the complex calculation that results in our being willing to make a commitment to another human being.

And twenty-five years as a couples therapist has taught me this: whatever the good stuff the two of you brought to your relationship, it's still there. I know that's sometimes hard to believe. When the anger and distance creep in, first you ignore it, then you try to fix things, then maybe you get mad on the outside but inside you're sad and scared, as if someone precious to you were very sick. But none of this helps.

The healing process would start immediately if we understood that, *It's not my spouse, it's not me, it's not us—it's our lives that are causing our problems. We're good people, we love each other, and there are still times when things are great between us. There's nothing wrong with our relationship deep down. We just have to figure out how to make things work between us when we don't have much time for each other.*

If this were how we approached each other—not looking at each other as the enemy but together facing a common enemy—the climate in our relationship would improve immediately. There would be less disappointment, more hope. We would know what to focus on, and it would be something that feels a lot better to deal with than those tired old who's-to-blame fights.

So now you know what to blame. The next time you find yourselves snapping at each other in the rush and pressure of your life, it might help to relieve the stress if you turn to your spouse and say, "That's the weekend marriage!"

The next time you start getting bummed out because it feels like you've grown too distant from each other, make yourselves feel better by saying, "That's the weekend marriage!"

The next time the two of you find yourselves mired in negativity and complaints, shift gears by saying, "That's the weekend marriage!"

The next time you sit down to talk about some issue and you both have good intentions but one word leads to another and you end up having the worst fight, remind yourself, "That's the weekend marriage!"

The next time in some mysterious way things somehow get cold and prickly and uncomfortable between you even though neither of you wants it to be this way, just tell yourselves, "That's the weekend marriage!"

IF YOU'RE A practical person like me, the minute you realize that it's living the weekend marriage that's hurting your relationship, you want to know, *Okay, so what can I do about it?*

We can't magically manufacture more time. Neither can we go on the way we've been, putting our relationships on a starvation diet.

At first I didn't have answers for how to fix this even in my own marriage, but this didn't let me off the hook. I've spent my professional life trying to find answers to problems like this. And I've learned to be optimistic. I was sure there were good answers out there. And eventually I found them.

The research we do at The Chestnut Hill Institute (where I'm clinical director) grows out of the belief that no matter what problems we struggle with, there are some people out there who've solved those problems. If we can just find those people and learn from them, we can get what we need to solve the same problems in our own lives.

I figured this must be true of the weekend marriage. So I looked at two groups of couples. They all lived the weekend marriage—there was no one living in the lap of leisure here. I asked everyone what living the weekend marriage was like for them. I wanted all the details.

People kept describing the weekend marriage by using words like *tense, rushed, businesslike, distant, irritated*. They'd talk about how phone calls, for example, were mostly brief, problem oriented, and not used as opportunities to get close. People generally didn't make love as often or as sensually as they wanted. It was people's sense that they frequently didn't kiss good-bye in the morning.

I kept hearing stories like these:

- "Lisa's mad at me because I come home so late. I always say I have so much work. But the truth is that I hang around the office because I'm so tired and I know that when I get home, there's going to be so much stuff to do and we'll eventually start getting on each other's nerves. Of course since I get home so late, we have even less time for each other."
- "I think we've been having this same fight for *weeks* now. We got mad at each other about something or other, but we have so little time to deal with anything, we've forgotten what the fight was about. We just know that we're mad at each other.

But we don't even remember what we need to deal with so we can resolve it."

- "When did Jake start picking on me the way he does? It's been an awfully long time. We both have so much on our plates and he needs me to be on top of things, but okay, I'm not a super-organized detail person like him. And we just fight about who's supposed to do what, and when. And then he wonders why I'm not interested in having sex with him."

- "We're never in sync. Rob gets home later than I do, but maybe he rests on the train—I don't know, but by nine o'clock he's gotten his second wind and wants us to start being to-gether. But by then I'm exhausted. I'm not good for anything. Then he thinks I'm either rejecting him or that he's married a dud. We fight about this all the time."

I kept looking for a way to understand what I was seeing. Shouldn't people who love each other, who'd taken the time to choose each other, who'd proven their ability to get along in the early stages of their relationship, have an easier time?

They do. I also talked to people who are doing just fine in spite of the weekend marriage. These successful couples didn't have a better fit or better genes or better luck or more money or anything else that the other couples or you or I don't have. So what made the difference?

THE SOLUTION

Chapter Four

THE SECRETS OF SUCCESSFUL WEEKEND-MARRIAGE COUPLES

Poor Jenny—she'd been in *two* weekend marriages! Both were similar in the sense that they'd both been relationships between two very busy people. Both had started with high hopes. In both marriages, Jenny could remember standing at the altar thinking, *I really love him. We fit so well together. This is going to be great!*

But the first had ended in the sad crash of divorce. The second, eight years in, still felt satisfying. Why?

Jenny echoes what other successful weekend-marriage couples said:

It strikes me now looking back on my first marriage how I did everything wrong but I thought I was doing everything right. At first I sacrificed myself for the sake of the relationship. Then I struggled with my husband over things because I thought that's what it meant to keep a relationship healthy. But that was exhausting and before long I stopped making even good things happen. As we got more frazzled, I started cutting my husband out of the loop. Just talking to him was so stressful. So I'd try to ignore things he did that annoyed me for as long as I could. But then at some point, of course, I'd reach my limit and I'd blow up at him. So we kept bouncing back and forth between big fights and too much distance. But I kept thinking it was all going to work out okay. I thought that if we just loved each other, the relationship would be there for us one day when we'd have more time. What a fool I was.

But now I'm doing things very differently in my second marriage.

I'm making sure I take excellent care of myself—you know, so I have something to give.

I've stopped doing things that could hurt our relationship. Given the way we live, there's no time to make a mess and then clean it up. What I have to do instead is focus on preventing damage. Besides, how can it be worthwhile to hurt the relationship just to make little tiny improvements in your spouse and yourself? This just destroys your ability to enjoy each other.

And I make it a priority to squeeze in as many good times as I can no matter what.

Overall I find that I'm more relaxed, less problem oriented, and more focused on the positive. All you can do is take care of yourself, enjoy things, and stop struggling over petty details. I think that's pretty good advice for couples trying to have a good relationship as we live our busy lives.

Jenny exemplifies what all the successful weekend-marriage people I interviewed have figured out:

> ### INSIGHT FOR ACTION
>
> Relationships die for lack of positive energy. This is the essential insight for finding abundant love in this time-starved world. Everything successful weekend-marriage couples do is designed to either create more positive energy or reduce negative energy.

A relationship is like a baby. A pediatrician will tell you that a baby is actually a pretty strong creature. But without nourishment it will die.

In the same way, couples living the time-starved lifestyle find that their relationship dies unless they feed it emotionally. This is because so many of the forces of the weekend marriage try to suck the energy out of it. The weekend marriage is not simply a normal relationship except with less time. It's a completely different kind of relationship because when we have much less time, we don't give to ourselves, we don't have time to give to each other, and the stresses we face make it easier for us to turn on each other.

We still love each other, but the distractions of our lives cause us to stop doing the things we know to do to take care of the relationship. Here's an illustration of how easy it is to get distracted. Just the other day a musician in Los Angeles accidentally left his million-dollar cello on his porch overnight (and of course it was gone the next morning). You might think this kind of thing never happens, but Yo-Yo Ma left his million-dollar cello on a train and concert violinist Gidon Kremer left *his* million-dollar Stradivarius in a cab. People can be just as careless with their relationships even though a good relationship is rarer and more precious than a great violin. It's stunning how easy it is to lose sight of what's most important when you're under pressure.

Now for the good news. You don't need *tons* of positive energy to keep your marriage healthy. Otherwise there would be very few successful weekend-marriage couples. You just need to give your relationship *some* positive energy, as long as it's enough to counteract the negative energy. And you have to do it consistently.

So what do successful weekend-marriage couples actually do?

I discovered that their methods consistently fit into the following four-part positive-energy strategy.

The first part is *taking care of yourself.* Successful weekend-marriage couples made it a priority to take care of themselves as individuals and made sure they each got their important needs met. It's paradoxical. Here they were in a relationship starved for time and attention, but they understood that unless they gave to themselves first, they wouldn't have any energy for each other. A little less for the relationship in the short run meant more for the relationship in the long run. Yes, it took time to give to themselves, but nothing good could happen in the relationship until they'd done something to take care of themselves. So this is the foundation.

The second part is *breaking free of your old patterns.* Successful weekend-marriage couples understood how demoralizing it is for you to find yourselves stuck in the same negative patterns, always getting into trouble with each other in the same way over and over again. These repetitive patterns destroy the hope that's necessary to build positive energy in your relationship, especially when you have so little time together. But when they learned how to block their old patterns, they freed up their time and their positive energy. This provided hope.

The third part of their energy strategy was *finding many different ways to get close, experience intimacy, and feel their love for each other in the limited time available.* It's not that they made it their priority to be together in any old way. They made it their priority to be together in *positive ways.* They proved that the quality of your time together is more important than the quantity. They found surprising ways to create positive energy even when under stress, even when they were angry with each other. This creates experiences of abundant love.

The fourth part of their energy strategy was *a commitment to not say or do anything that would injure their relationship.* Of course no one wants to hurt their relationship. But most weekend-marriage couples fail to protect their relationship. It's not because they don't care. It's just because they don't know what else to do. And when they've come home late or they're tired or they realize their spouse forgot to pay a bill that's now way overdue, taking care of the relationship always comes in second. But this is bad for the health of the relationship.

Successful weekend-marriage couples understand that there is only a fixed amount of energy to work with. Every bit of negative energy—energy tied up in anger or frustration or coldness—means there's that much less positive energy.

This is why successful couples made protecting their relationship from injury a top priority. They figured out how to best deal with each other when they were stressed out, how to minimize impatience and irritability, and how to protect themselves from getting sucked into painful conflicts. Less damage to the relationship meant more opportunities to enjoy each other.

THIS FOUR-PART positive-energy strategy gave successful weekend-marriage couples everything they needed not just to survive the time crunch but to thrive in spite of it. And that's *all* you'll need. You've passed the no-time-for-love test. When the two of you have time together, things are better. In the land of love, you're a good fit. Your love is alive even if it's been a while since it made your toes curl. You still have everything you need to create abundant love.

Remember when the idea *Just be yourself* worked in your relationship? This four-part strategy will bring you back to that time. The help here isn't designed to change you. It's just designed to help you integrate your free, natural, easy, self-trusting pre-weekend-marriage selves within the realities of your time-starved lives.

When you do this, you can fulfill your dream of having a great relationship. For most of us, one of the hallmarks of a great relationship is that it's filled with mutual honesty. Yes, honesty can be tough to take sometimes. But honesty is the soil out of which true intimacy grows. That's why mutual honesty is so important. Not as an abstract moral principle. But because of its power to create deeper, longer-lasting intimacy. That's the *kind* of honesty you and I want. Not the barren kind where you have two people hurling angry truths at each other, and when the other person gets hurt they say, "Hey, I was just being honest." But the fertile honesty that brings forth more honesty, where both people feel safe sharing their thoughts and feelings, where both feel accepted for who they are, and where this sharing helps them achieve true intimacy.

TAKING CARE
OF YOURSELF

Chapter Five

RECHARGING YOUR BATTERIES

Every night on her drive home from work Susan passes the exit that goes to the airport. And every night as she approaches that exit Susan has fantasies of yanking the steering wheel to the right, driving into the airport, and hopping on the first plane that will take her very far away.

Of course Susan would never actually do this. She loves her husband and she loves her kids. Besides, Susan's the soul of responsibility. She told me that it was unimaginable to her that she would actually do anything as crazy and hurtful as running off like that.

So why does Susan feel a little disappointed in herself every time she doesn't take that exit? It's because it represents something she desperately needs—to get away from it all, to stop feeling so overwhelmed, to go somewhere where she can finally, utterly relax.

Like everyone living the weekend marriage, it's all too much for Susan. The pace of her life is such that Susan can rarely catch her breath. She's surrounded by people who seem to want to suck her dry. Of course no one would put it that way. Work is just a place where things have to get done. And the kids aren't especially "needy"; they're just kids. And her husband, Gregg, is a full-grown adult—so why should she think of him as being full of needs?

But that's how it all feels to Susan. Gregg's always needing to talk to her about what needs to get done. He's needing her to listen to the problems he's having at work. He's needing to explain some theory he has about something that's going on somewhere in the world. He's needing her to treat him with kid gloves, as if his frayed nerves were the most important thing in the world.

How could anyone meet all the needs of all these people? But Susan tries. Every morning, every night she resolves that she's going to be the good, caring, efficient person she wants to be. But too often she ends up disappointed in herself. As she's rushing around in the evening, Gregg suddenly asks, "Where's the newspaper?" and Susan loses it. She snaps at him as if he'd committed a terrible crime: "You have eyes. What am I, your mother? Look for it yourself."

In a way, Gregg did do something terrible, though not intentionally, of course: he asked for something from someone who had nothing left to give. And so one more time the monster was given an opportunity to rise up out of the depths of the weekend marriage and attack people's abilities to love each other.

Susan's instincts were right about hopping on a plane. It's not that running away from her family is the right thing to do. But she's right about needing to recharge her batteries. This is one of the most important ingredients for successfully living the week-end marriage.

INSIGHT FOR ACTION

You can't give to your spouse unless you have some-thing to give. So you have to make sure that you recharge your batteries by doing something to relax, feed your soul, quiet your jangled emotions, and feel like yourself again. And you have to do it first.

Imagine that. Your relationship is starved for time and yet the first thing you have to do is allocate some of that oh-so-scarce time to your need to relax and take care of yourself.

But it makes enormous sense. Just think about it. The less time you have together, the more important it is to have high-quality time together. And so paradoxically you must spend even less time together if that's what it takes to make sure that the quality of your time together feels better. How can you have a great rela-tionship when what you're bringing to the table is someone who's stretched to the max and has nothing to give?

Suppose the shoe were on the other foot. Suppose your spouse came to you and said, "Honey, with all the pressure and running around I've been doing, I've got nothing to offer right now. We could be together now but wouldn't you rather I recharged my batteries first so that when we're together in an hour or tomor-row I have something to give?"

What would you say? That you'd prefer an extra hour with someone who has nothing to give or less time with someone who has something to give. I know which *I'd* choose.

And you've done this kind of thing already. Remember when you were first dating? *You'd cancel a date if you were grumpy and exhausted from work.* You'd do that because you knew how dangerous it was *not* to do that.

Yet we flirt with danger every time we interact without having done something first to recharge our batteries. All that's worst about us is at risk of coming out. At the slightest irritation or disappointment, we lose it. And when we let the other person have it, we'll say we're telling the truth about how we feel, but if we're really honest with ourselves, we're giving truth a bad name. This isn't authentic honesty. It's just what honesty looks like when we're so frazzled and frayed and feel so deprived that we'll say anything. We'll direct toward our spouses feelings that aren't really reactions to anything they did and have little to do with who they are.

As one man put it, "Most of the time when I go off like that, those aren't my authentic feelings. That's me taking the irritations of the day and throwing them at my wife's head. Sometimes I get mad not because the issue is real but just so she'll leave me the hell alone."

So which do you think is better for your relationship? Making the decision to recharge your batteries? Or putting yourself in a situation where you'll almost certainly end up having a fight with your spouse?

Now you might have a very sensible question at this point. Here I am making a big deal about how no one has any time anymore and yet I'm telling you that you need to take some time for yourself. How can you do it?

All I can say is that people do it every day. Time-management consultants tell me that you can always find time for your highest priorities if you dump some lower priorities. I don't know the details of your life. But I'd bet anything that you're spending time busy with stuff that's *way* less necessary for you than recharging your batteries.

Suppose you *don't* do this. Suppose you keep dragging yourself through your relationship always running on empty. Do you think you won't pay a price for that? This is how weekend marriages end up in the divorce courts. Just think about it. If you have two people interacting who have nothing to give but are still needing to get something from each other, they'll end up angry and disappointed. If you've ever experimented with trying to get by on significantly less sleep *(sleeping is such a waste—think of how much more I could get done if I slept two hours less a night)*, you know what a disaster it usually is to go day after day with your batteries not fully charged.

THE EXCUSE THAT many people use for not recharging their batteries is that they can't afford to do what it would take. This is the two-weeks-on-a-beach-in-the-Bahamas-or-else fallacy. But the truth is that it doesn't take a major escape from your life to recharge your battery. You may be surprised at how little it takes. I know one hard-charging guy who solved the problem by buying a bicycle and going for a half-hour spin around the neighborhood every evening.

You know how when you're really, really hungry you think you can eat a ton of food but it turns out that after eating three quarters of a sandwich, you're full? It's the same with recharging your batteries. That's why Susan understood that she didn't have to hop on a plane and escape from her life. That would've been like saying, "I could eat a horse," and then actually sitting down and trying to eat a whole horse. Whoa!

Over and over when I ask people what they do to recharge their batteries, the things they say work best for them are little things. For example, after his drive home in the evening, one guy I know pulls into his garage, turns off the car, and just sits there for five or ten minutes. Sometimes he even lets himself doze off. He tries to relax every muscle in his body, as if by doing that he's letting go of all the tensions that have built up during the day and allowing himself to feel completely renewed.

Little things are best, because when we're living the weekend marriage, we get drained on an almost daily basis. You can prove to yourself that this is true. Think about the last time you returned completely refreshed from a two-week vacation. How many days back at work did it take for the pressure to take hold again? Two days? One day?

Needing to recharge your batteries on an almost-daily basis is a reason why little things work best.

It's important to recharge your batteries *before* you get together with your spouse. If you put it off until the last thing in the evening, it might be great for you but it's not that much help to your relationship.

Here are some other things lots of people do to recharge their batteries. There are no big surprises here, but if these suggestions stimulate you to come up with your perfect personal idea for how you can recharge your batteries, they'll have served their purpose.

Swim laps at a local pool.
Take a yoga class.

Have a nap.

Chat with a supportive, upbeat friend.

Soak in a tub.

Get a massage.

Go for a run.

Attend a religious service.

Meditate.

Listen to music.

Take a dog for a walk.

Dance until you've worked up a sweat.

Eat a quiet lunch by yourself.

Or do anything else that's worked in the past or that you think might work and that you can squeeze into your busy day. It doesn't matter what you do. It just matters that it's a way for you to give to yourself, that you've chosen it, and that it leaves you feeling refreshed. The themes that keep coming up are solitude, rest, creativity, and connecting with others.

If you're ever stumped for a way to recharge your batteries, just close your eyes and say, "You know what would be really nice now? If I could just . . ." Whatever comes into your mind, do that.

The point is that this is not only a gift you're giving to yourself, but it's also something essential that you're doing for your relationship. Try it. Watch how when you bring a more nurtured self into your relationship, your relationship is more nurturing to you.

Guerrilla tactics. (From time to time throughout this book I'm going to offer special guerrilla tactics for doing things to improve the health of your weekend marriage. I call them guerrilla tactics because I understand that they're not for everyone. Some may find a few of them too radical. But I recommend them because they *work* and they work fast. So feel free to use any of these guerrilla tactics. If your first reaction is: *Oh, I could never do that,* ask yourself if you're sure. And if you are sure, feel free to leave it alone.)

In case there's any doubt, I really am saying that you should do *whatever* it takes to bring your best self to your relationship. A relationship that's starved for time is like a person who's starved for food. He's not just hungry. He's weakened. Feeding him junk food at a time like that could make him sick. The weaker he is, the more important it is that he have only the best.

Joan was a trial lawyer. She went through a period in her life during which she was, she claimed, "the busiest person who ever lived, bar none." She could count the time she could spend with her husband during the past month in minutes at best. Then she saw light at the end of the tunnel. There was the possibility she could take some well-deserved time off. Naturally, her husband said, "Let's go on vacation together." Even though she missed him terribly, she was surprised to find that the idea didn't excite her. In fact, it depressed her.

Finally she admitted the truth to herself. She didn't want to go on vacation with her husband. Lots of times our greatest hunger is for connection. But sometimes our greatest hunger is for silence, peace, and solitude. That's the state Joan was in. And it's never more important than when you're living the stress of the weekend marriage to pay serious attention to your greatest needs.

So Joan thought of a compromise. She said to her husband, "Honey, I love you madly but I need a week to myself before I'm fit company for anyone. Join me after the first week and we'll have a great week together after that." Joan felt terribly guilty as she flew toward the Caribbean by herself. But the first three days she was there, she never even left her hotel room. She saw how desperately she'd been needing to recharge her batteries.

What a difference it made. The Joan that greeted her husband at the airport after a week of rest and peace was a Joan that had come back to life. She was ready for fun, for giving love to someone else, and for receiving love from someone else (because even that's too much when your batteries are drained). They could reconnect, make love, have long conversations, but only because Joan had taken care of herself first.

Joan's story makes an important point. Recharging your batteries is so important for your relationship that you may need to do something as radical as taking your own vacation before you go on vacation with your spouse. Or figuring out a way to take a whole vacation by yourself if you need it. You can take a minivacation and stay in bed over a long weekend. You can take a permanent vacation from making the beds or doing other chores that use up your time and give you little back.

The point isn't what you do. The point is doing whatever it takes to recharge your batteries. That's the guerrilla tactic here.

Now let's deal with the main excuses for why we don't give to ourselves.

I'm already taking care of myself. Many people get their priorities screwed up when they try to take care of themselves.

Sometimes we fall victim to the vending-machine syndrome— you know, eating a candy bar when you're hungry because the vending machine is right there even when a candy bar isn't what you want or need. We do this when we're low on energy by letting convenience drive what we do to take care of ourselves. For example, one guy would always stop off at the bar for a couple of beers on the way home from work. The bar was right on his way and the parking lot always had room. It's not that he enjoyed it so much. But it was there.

And sometimes it's all about how tired we are. We think we're recharging our batteries when we collapse in front of the TV at the end of the day. But nothing gets recharged. It's just a way to exist in a low-energy state.

If you think you're already recharging your batteries, ask yourself, *What could I do that would truly renew, refresh, revitalize me?* And then do *that*.

There's always tomorrow or next week. To prevent damage to your relationship, you need to recharge your batteries when you *start* feeling you have nothing to give. If you wait until tomorrow or next week, you won't realize you've run out of juice until you find yourself picking a fight with your spouse or doing something to distance yourself. Either way, you hurt your relationship and delay the possibility of something good happening.

You can take time for yourself today without a fight, without blowing up, without a big mess, without being too needy yourself. Or you can take time for yourself tomorrow, when you've been pushed to the limit and then need not only to take time for yourself but also to heal a huge fight.

Think about it: we don't drive until we run out of gas. We figure we're going to have to stop at some point, so we stop before it's too late. If we wait until we run out, it's a big hassle to walk to find a gas station.

So say to yourself, *If I wait until tomorrow, the delay might cause real harm.*

But I have no idea what to do to recharge my batteries. It's so often the case in life that we know we need something but we don't know what it is. However, it's a very big mistake to say that if you don't know what you need, then you don't have a need. Accept as true that you need to recharge your batteries. Don't let not knowing how to recharge them let you off the hook.

Then say to yourself, *I may not know a great thing to do to replenish myself yet. But I do know some things that would help me a little and I'll do those things until I can come up with something better.*

I'd feel very selfish if I went off to do something for myself when everyone in my family is so busy and has so many needs. I know from personal experience that this is a tough excuse to get out of. Who wants to deal with a spouse's disappointment? Who wants to be labeled *selfish?* But this takes a short-term view.

And remember, you're not Superman. When people don't do what they need to do to recharge their batteries, it's not that they collapse in a heap. It's more likely that resentment, depression, and plain old exhaustion cause them to stop giving. People running on empty pour negative energy into their relationships.

That's when people either collapse, make stupid decisions, or act mean. The more generous you want to be, the more you need to recharge your batteries so you can be truly effective.

You know there really are lazy, selfish people. But if this is something you're worried about, then you're probably not one of these people. The main way to check for this is to ask yourself what your spouse would say. Would your spouse say he'd prefer that you keep on pushing yourself or that first you do what you need to do so later you have something to give?

Say to yourself, *If I don't take care of myself right now, I won't be able to take care of others.* Say to your spouse, "I need to do this for myself so I'll have something to give to you." Present your need to recharge your batteries as a way of being more loving, more present, and more generous in your relationship.

BUILDING HOPE

Chapter Six

BREAKING FREE OF YOUR OLD PATTERNS

Have you ever noticed how the monster stalking your relationship is really boring? Destructive and demoralizing, sure, but boring. There you and your spouse are, wanting nothing more than some sweet lovin'. Then you find yourselves having the same argument in the same way about the same thing as you always do.

You can't have positive energy for your relationship without the hope that things will get better, and how can you have this hope if no matter how hard you try, you always have the same fight and end up in the same unhappy place? You'd think the monster would get creative, but he always seems to mess you up in exactly the same way. The only thing that ever really varies is what starts the fight.

- John and Gail are both very opinionated people. When they had to deal with a plumber who came to fix a burst pipe, John wanted to handle it but Gail had a lot of opinions about how

John could be handling it better. *"What's wrong with you?"* John said at one point. *"What's wrong with me?"* Gail said, *"I'm not the one who's a complete idiot."* And every fight went like this, a barroom brawl that seemed to come out of nowhere.

- Ann and Zeke are nice, polite people. One year Zeke forgot Ann's birthday. Ann said sadly, *"I'm very disappointed,"* but when Zeke seemed upset at having forgotten, she added, *"Don't worry about it."* But there was a chill. Neither of them wanted to talk about it. The chill continued. It was always like this— someone getting disappointed and not dealing with it.

- When Will went to buy a new car, he'd agreed with Sandi on a price limit. But when he pulled into the driveway with his new SUV, Sandi had a sinking feeling and asked, *"How much did this cost us?"* Will said, *"It was around what we'd agreed."* Sandi demanded to see the paperwork. It was ten thousand dollars more than they'd agreed. Sandi was furious. For a long time Will didn't say anything; then he started criticizing Sandi for getting so upset: *"Why do you always have to go crazy like this?"* Will said. As usual, Sandi was the angry one (according to Will) and Will was the jerk (according to Sandi) who refused to deal with her when she got mad.

If you want to understand why couples keep having the same fight over and over, you have to start with the way people deal with each other when they're under pressure. The kind of fights you get into come from the kind of people you are. A person is either a *confronter* or an *avoider*. It doesn't matter what kind of person you are at work, or what kind of person you think you are, or what kind of person you were in previous relationships. We're just talking about whether you're a confronter or an avoider in your relationship right now.

You are someone who tends to *confront* in your current relationship if four or more of the following statements apply to you:

1. You hate to keep things bottled up.
2. You have a short fuse.
3. You're not afraid of conflict.
4. You believe in telling it like it is.
5. You're usually the first in your relationship to bring up problems.
6. You think it can be healthy for a couple to fight.
7. If someone says something to you that makes you mad, you're likely to come right back at them.

You are someone who tends to *avoid confrontation* in your current relationship if four or more of the following statements apply to you:

1. You hate conflict.
2. You're reluctant to bring up problems.
3. Even though you think you shouldn't, you tend to keep your feelings to yourself.
4. It upsets you when things aren't nice between you and your spouse.
5. When your spouse gets mad, you try to calm him down or get away from him.
6. You hope that if you just leave problems alone they'll sort themselves out.

7. When your spouse is mad at you, she often labels you as "silent" or "unemotional."

Don't take the words *confronter* or *avoider* as either a compliment or an insult. They're just descriptive. So let's use *dog* and *duck*. I happen to think that dogs and ducks are both wonderful animals. But they are different. A dog will snap at you if he feels challenged—dogs just don't hide how they feel. A duck will . . . well, a duck will duck confrontation. He'll fly or swim away. So from now on if you're a confronter, I'll call you a dog. And if you're an avoider, I'll call you a duck. Okay?

And now you're ready to discover your couple style. There are really only three. One couple style isn't better than another. They're just different. But if you see which style you fall into, you'll know how you keep getting into trouble and how to prevent it. The three patterns come from whether you and your spouse are dogs (confronters) or ducks (avoiders).

Here are the three patterns of weekend marriages:

1. If you both tend to confront each other when one does something the other dislikes, you're in a *dog/dog relationship.* There are a lot of explosions.
2. If you both tend to avoid confrontations, you're in a *duck/duck relationship.* There's a lot of silence and distance.
3. If one of you tends to confront and the other avoid, you're in a *dog/duck relationship.* There's frustration and disappointment.

Which style is yours? (You might also want to amuse yourself by guessing your friends' styles.) As you see more of the three styles, you'll get a clearer sense of where you fit in. It might help to understand that people don't fit perfectly neatly into pure types. And your style might have been different in the past. But this is about the way you usually deal with conflict now. When you see which is your style, it's crucial that you acknowledge it. Only then will you be able to stay out of the kind of trouble your style falls into.

ENDING THE EXPLOSIONS: DOG/DOG RELATIONSHIPS

Carly and Dave came to me because they'd gotten into a fight so bad that they'd scared the crap out of themselves. Two intense individuals who are both more than ready to stand up for themselves almost always end up in this place. And they get here much sooner if they're squeezed by the stresses of the weekend marriage.

There'd been so many fights before, always starting with Carly or Dave saying something like, "I'm so sick of the way you . . . ," or, "You're lazy and selfish and you need to wake up." Needless to say, the other didn't respond by apologizing. Just the opposite. The response was more like "What are you, nuts? I give everything I have to this relationship and you do nothing. I must've been crazy to think I could be married to you." Kitchen utensils had been flung across the room. Photographs torn up. Walls punched.

This time, though, it had been worse. They'd both been under a lot of pressure at work. And you know how it is—the more you feel under the gun, the more you put pressure on your spouse to help you out, leave you alone, take care of business, do whatever it takes to ease the pressure on you.

One morning, at the last minute, Carly asked Dave to drive her to the airport. Maxed-out himself, Dave gave her a hard time. It would make him late for work, specially with all the traffic. Carly talked about how a cab to the airport costs a fortune, which wouldn't matter so much if Dave were making more money. The fighting escalated in the car. Before they knew it, Carly was punching Dave in the arm and he was punching the steering wheel. When they pulled up at the airport, Dave meant to give Carly a slight shove as she got out of the car, as if to say, *If you're in such a rush, here, let me help you,* but something went wrong and he shoved just hard enough so that she fell down and scraped her knee in front of everyone.

That's when they knew they were in trouble. This incident was like all the other blowups they'd lived through. It was just worse, and so it served as a nightmarish warning of the kinds of blowups they might expect in the future.

Naturally each blamed the other for being impulsive, provocative, hotheaded, and irresponsible. They missed the real problem. Carly and Dave were in a *dog/dog relationship*. That's what you get when two people come together who can't help responding with full emotional intensity to whatever their spouse puts out. One gets mad, the other gets mad. One yells, the other yells. One insults, the other insults. And so dog/dog relationships, as you can imagine, are characterized by extreme volatility.

Don't get me wrong. These couples aren't fighting all the time. It's just that any small disagreement can and often does rapidly escalate into a big explosion.

Sometimes couples don't realize they are in this type of marriage because when they're first going out together, nothing much happens to provoke a confrontation. No wonder. The time they spend dating is relatively stress free. But our time-starved lifestyle can quickly reveal the dog/dog couple. When they're under the gun, they will confront each other. And they won't back down; they'll just raise the stakes.

Every marriage is an attempt by two people to build a bridge connecting them. The kinds of pressures that accompany the weekend marriage will reveal the hidden cracks in this bridge— every fundamental disagreement, every difference in how two people like to live. In a dog/dog relationship every crack leads to an explosion. The more pressure, the more cracks, the more explosions.

You know you're in a dog/dog relationship if you keep having huge fights that seem to come out of nowhere and get real ugly real fast. Does this sound like your relationship?

If you're in a dog/dog relationship, you have to stop blaming your spouse. Oh sure, if he or she were perfect, you wouldn't have any problems. But everyone in every relationship is imperfect. It's not you and your spouse's imperfections that create this volatile dynamic. It's your willingness, even eagerness, to confront back when each of you feels you've been confronted. You're not enemies. You're partners in a dance. But it's a dance where one of you brings the gasoline and the other brings matches. The way the monster crawls out of the weekend marriage to get you is through your volatility.

Once you end the blame game, you can see the dynamics of the dog/dog relationship:

The *strength* of this type is that few important issues are lurking in the dark. There tend to be few secrets. What you see is what you get. You know what's going on with each other. Because both people are bluntly honest, a lot of good information comes out. Interestingly, there's a lot of trust in this type (unless the volatility has led to violence) because of both people's inability to keep secret for very long what's going on inside them.

The *weakness* of this type of relationship is that enormous amounts of time can be spent fighting and recovering from fights. And you never know when some small spark will set off a huge conflagration. Because you're afraid of blowups, you can feel as if you're walking on eggshells much of the time until the inevitable confrontation explodes. These relationships can be exhausting. And they're particularly vulnerable to the stresses that come with the weekend marriage.

The *risk* of this type of relationship is that your volatility will blow your marriage out of the water. This can happen in two ways. Sometimes you just go too far. One of you says something unforgivable. One of you does something he or she regrets. Something gets broken. Even if there's not physical violence, there's such a scary level of anger that eventually one or both of you feel you have to get out. Sometimes, though, it ends not with a bang but with a whimper. You're so exhausted from so many big fights that you need a divorce just to get back some of your emotional energy.

The *opportunity* if you're in a dog/dog relationship is that you can have a very vital and intense relationship with a great deal of mutual honesty if you can just find a way to control your potential for volatility. The good news is that this is very do-able, even if you've never done it before.

Here's how to succeed with this couple style:

INSIGHT FOR ACTION

Since all the problems in a dog/dog relationship come from dangerous escalation, what this type of couple needs most is a braking mechanism, a way to stop the volatility. If couples were cars, these couples would need a brake pedal.

To get the brake pedal, you need to make an unshakeable agreement that *stop means stop.* You know that you get into trouble because you let small disagreements turn into big fights. So if you both agree that stop means stop, then you're both safe. After all, you're not stupid—you know how badly you've been hurt by not having this brake.

I know what you're thinking. *We've never been able to stop our fights.* Sure, and that's because your desire to win your fights has been more important to you than your understanding of how dangerous this dynamic is. And each person in a dog/dog couple always wants to get in the last word.

But people change lots of things in their lives when they realize the dangers. Plus, this isn't one of you trying to shut the other up—you know how successful *that's* been. This is the two of you following through on an agreement that you've made together.

Here's how you work it. When the fighting and anger start to flare, as soon as you can think of it, one of you says *stop* and then both of you respect that and stop. Now you're not going to want to stop. You wouldn't be a dog/dog couple if you did want to stop, anymore than you'd be a race car driver if you enjoyed braking. But you do stop, because you know that your volatility means that every fight points you straight toward the danger zone.

In my experience, most dog/dog couples can learn to keep to the stop-means-stop agreement. And that's good, because when they can't keep to the agreement, their volatility almost always leads to their breaking up.

Of course you don't stop forever. You just stop until the next day, or until you're both calmed down, or until you both agree to *calmly discuss* whatever you were fighting about. It's important to recognize that you will soon be able to pick up the issue again. It's only feeling safe from your volatility that makes intimacy possible. How can you both speak from the heart if you don't feel safe?

Suppose Carly and Dave had done this on their drive to the airport. After Carly said, *"I'm so sick of how you're never there for me,"* or after Dave said, *"You're so selfish and demanding,"* one of them would've said, *Wait a minute,* stop. *Remember our agreement— whoever says* stop, *we both stop. If we don't stop this now, we both know where it's going to lead.* And then the other would've said, *Okay.*

That's all it takes. You may feel disoriented at the sudden halt in the fight. It feels weird to go from the familiarity of intense confrontation straight into silence. But remember: you're just preventing an explosion; you're not foreclosing a discussion of the issues. And you're saving your love from the monster.

You never again have to experience your volatility. What you can experience is a level of safety you've not had before. And it means that you now have a much greater chance of experiencing abundant love. Even though you don't have much time together, the time you do have is safer, happier, and more satisfying.

Because it's so targeted to your situation, *stop means stop* may be the only tool you need to prevent those fights that occur over and over in your relationship. What a time-saver!

ENDING THE SILENCE: DUCK/DUCK RELATIONSHIPS

How can I show you a duck/duck relationship? What you see looks so normal on the surface that you might think there are no problems. At most you see two people having a polite conversation. The thing is that *all there is* is polite conversation. Real disagreements might be brought up, but then they're dealt with in a strange way. Either the individuals quickly reach an agreement that doesn't address their real underlying issues or they distract each other with irrelevant comments and end up not dealing with anything at all.

You can still be a duck even though you're a hard charger at work. Plenty of people are aggressive go-getters professionally but mild ducks in their marriages. They just hate confrontations with the person they love.

I said it's hard to show a duck/duck relationship. But it's not so hard to explain what it feels like to be in one.

There's a cool, calm, polite surface. You almost never fight; you just have occasional long "discussions" that go nowhere and resolve nothing. There can be a lot of silences. Your spouse's sure that he's brought up problems from time to time, but you can't remember his having said anything.

Below the surface, though, there's a sad sense of distance and of frustration over unmet needs. Does this sound like your relationship?

It's interesting how the weekend marriage plays into this. The same pressures of a fast-paced lifestyle that lead to explosions for dog/dog couples are a perfect excuse for duck/duck couples to avoid their issues. Hey, there's no time!

The *strength* of a duck/duck relationship is that on a day-to-day basis the two of you have caused little damage to each other. No horrible insults you'd love to take back. And you haven't used up your precious time dealing with problems.

The *weakness* of a duck/duck relationship is that important issues are not being dealt with. Crucial information is hidden. There are likely to be real problems festering below the surface. The politeness you see can be a mask for anger, even despair. When a problem does surface, people in this kind of relationship use their energy not to solve the problem but to get out of talking about the problem with their spouse. They'll probably talk to their friends instead of talking to their spouse about what's bothering them.

The *risk* of being in a duck/duck relationship is that if problems aren't dealt with, they usually grow. And as problems grow, anger grows. All this happens below the surface. Soon people grow incredibly distant. There's not only little honesty about the important issues, there's little emotional juice to bring people closer. Sometimes this can go so far that the relationship dies before anyone acknowledges there was a problem. Another risk is that people will deal with their issues or needs by going outside the relationship. Lots of people in duck/duck relationships have affairs.

The *opportunity* if you're in a duck/duck relationship is that your politeness and fear of confrontation can be a huge strength if you force yourselves to deal with the real issues between you. If any two people can have those reasonable discussions that all couples hope for, it's you two.

Here's what you need to succeed with this couple style:

INSIGHT FOR ACTION

Since most problems in a duck/duck relationship come from not dealing with problems, the greatest need for this type of couple is for them to deal with what they've been avoiding. They need to open their mouths and bare their souls. If couples were cars, duck/duck couples need a gas pedal.

To get the "gas pedal," a duck/duck couple needs to hold *a weekly meeting.* Holding this weekly meeting will be a sacred obligation. Standing appointments are one of the classic ways people have for getting themselves to do things that they're not instinctively inclined to do. I don't always like to exercise, but if I'm scheduled to play tennis with someone every Monday morning at seven, I have to be there or I'll let that person down. The appointment compensates for my tendency to want to stay in bed longer on Monday mornings.

The weekly meeting should take place when you have a little free time. Most couples prefer to have it on the weekend. At the weekly meeting you each have an obligation to bring up one problem in your relationship. Then you both have an obligation to respond honestly, have an open discussion, and come to some kind of agreement. I know I've talked about getting away from having a problem-oriented relationship. But even if problems are no longer the focus, they still rear their ugly heads from time to time. Better to set aside a time for dealing with them than to have problem talk leak into the rest of your lives.

It can go something like this. Jackie says how she feels about some issue, such as, "I'm sad that we haven't been having much sex recently." Then she says what she needs: "I'd like us to go back to having sex a couple of times a week." Stating her need is an important step, because without it the feeling can just sound like a complaint. Then she offers something that she feels might be a solution: "Let's try having sex in the morning, since we both get up early and we're always so tired in the evening."

But duck/duck couples have to be careful now. Tom has to say how he feels, what he needs, and what solution he'd like. This is important because when they're faced with solutions they're not comfortable with, ducks either confuse the issue or make an agreement they're not going to keep.

This solution creates more mutual honesty. If you and I are talking about where to go out for dinner and I say, "Let's have some Chinese food," I have to be saying that because it's what I really want. But if you agree to it even though you're sick of Chinese food, then one of us is going to be unhappy with the dinner. But if you say, "Oh gosh, I'm so sick of Chinese food. It's all I've been eating," then maybe it will turn out that your first choice, Italian food, is my second choice. We're both happy! And that could only happen because we made it possible for both of us to be honest about what we want. But to get to that honest place we have to get past that awkward moment where you're uncomfortable saying how you really feel.

Using the weekly meeting improves things for duck/duck couples because they tend to use lack of time as an excuse for avoiding dealing with problems. What's the worst that can happen? That when you start out you'll seem to be very far apart on some issue? So what? Most successful negotiations start out with two people who seem very far apart. *It's the willingness to negotiate, not the distance between the initial positions, that predicts a successful outcome.*

Let's get back to Jackie and Tom. Maybe Tom doesn't feel that having sex in the morning deals with his real issue. Maybe he's been really tired. Maybe he's angry about something. Maybe something's making it hard for him to initiate sex. But once he says how he feels, he can put out his need, such as, "It feels like every time we talk about anything these days, you're so businesslike, it puts me off and makes me mad. I don't know how to connect with you in a sexual way. I need you to act a little warm and sexy and vulnerable."

Then he proposes his solution. Hopefully it's something that fits in with her solution: *"Yeah, I think having sex in the morning is a good idea. But it will make all the difference to me if you'd try to act a little softer when you're wanting us to make love."*

Putting forth needs like this moves the duck/duck couple toward more openness. The world doesn't end when there's a disagreement. If you find that you can't agree in the time you have, you have to resolve it in the next weekly meeting.

Because it's so targeted to your situation, holding a weekly

meeting may be the only tool you need to prevent those difficulties that occur over and over in your relationship. What a
time-saver!

ENDING THE DISAPPOINTMENT: DOG/DUCK RELATIONSHIPS

What happens when a dog meets a duck? The dog chases the
duck. But the duck usually has no problem getting away. If you
had a dog and a duck locked in a big old barn, the dog could be
chasing the duck and the duck could be escaping the dog forever.

How does this apply to weekend-marriage couples? What does
it even mean for one person to be "chasing" another? And why
are they chasing each other?

Karen and Steve have a typical dog/duck relationship.

Karen wears her heart on her sleeve. When she feels something,
she says it with as much intensity as she feels it. If something's
bothering her, the danger and dishonesty that she feels go along
with being silent are almost physically painful to her. Karen's the
dog in their relationship.

Steve hates confrontations, scenes, emotionality. It all embar-
rasses him, makes him very uncomfortable. He wouldn't admit it,
but he actually gets scared when someone gets mad at him. He
thinks too many people make too much of a big deal about too
many things. Steve's the duck.

Now here's how Karen ends up chasing Steve around the barn.

Steve thinks he's a nice, peaceful, reasonable guy. Karen knows
that he's basically a good guy, but come on—he's not perfect.
Even a saint would do things to annoy her. And Steve's no saint.

Karen thinks she's honest, open, and well meaning. She just wants to stand up for herself and keep their relationship healthy. But in her attempts to be honest and bring up issues, she can seem like a troublemaker to Steve.

Steve does something that's just as provocative to Karen when she confronts him: he tries to get out of talking about it. Steve has a dozen tricks up his sleeve. He pretends not to hear. Heck, maybe he really doesn't hear confrontational comments. Or he agrees to whatever Karen's going blah, blah, blah about and then immediately forgets the agreement. Perhaps his most provocative tactic is to comment on the manner Karen uses to talk to him rather than on the specific issue Karen's bringing up: "Okay, but why do you have to get so upset about this?" Steve says.

The next thing you know they're having two parallel, disconnected arguments. Steve's talking about *how* Karen says what she says. Karen's just struggling to have her point heard. Of course being opposed and not listened to like this just makes Karen angrier. Which she shows. Which just makes Steve all the more reluctant to deal with her.

That's how dog/duck couples end up chasing each other all around the barn.

From the dog's point of view, the duck will seem passive-aggressive, scared, stupid, evasive, irresponsible, immature, or unreliable. It will seem to the dog as though it's impossible to get the duck to deal in a real way with an important issue.

But from the duck's point of view, the dog is crazy, angry, troublemaking, bullying, petty, overinvolved, and perfectionistic. It seems to ducks that dogs will say and do things they don't mean just to get their spouses to engage with them.

The result of this endless chase around the barn is disappointment. At bottom Karen is disappointed in Steve. He hears what she says. Why doesn't he deal with it? And Steve is disappointed in Karen. Okay, she has things she wants to talk to him about. So why does she have to spoil it by going so far and making it such a big deal when it would be so easy to have a calm discussion?

You know you're in a dog/duck relationship if what you see over and over is the confronter trying to engage the avoider but the avoider being uncomfortable and trying to duck out of it. Does this sound like your relationship?

The weekend marriage intensifies this dynamic. Exhausted and pressed for time, dogs are more easily provoked and more likely to express disappointment in a confrontational way. Ducks are more likely to be fed up with any attempt at confrontation.

The *strength* of a dog/duck relationship is that one person brings problem-solving energy to the relationship and the other refuses to let anger escalate. You can see the potential here for this couple to be a great team.

The *weakness* of a dog/duck relationship comes from the way fights constantly shift from the issue at hand to who the other person is. This gives full rein to the monster because their disappointment in each other makes them feel badly about themselves for being in the relationship. This type more than the other two is at risk of feeling that they don't belong together.

The *risk* of being in a dog/duck relationship is that one or both get so tired of chasing or being chased, of being disappointed in the other, of never connecting in the same way about the same issue, that they may give up on the relationship.

The *opportunity* if you're in a dog/duck relationship is that *you're close to a great solution.* The dog and the duck can work well together. They just have to stop the chase. And they're close to a solution because it's not talking about problems in itself that scares the duck; it's the atmosphere of confrontation. And a lot of the things the dog was doing that seemed so confrontational were just attempts to get the duck's attention. When you have one person saying, "I'll stop running away if you'll stop chasing me," and the other person saying, "I'll stop chasing you if you stop running away," then you know you're tantalizingly close to a solution.

Here's what you need to succeed with this relationship pattern:

INSIGHT FOR ACTION

The problems in a dog/duck relationship come from disappointment that the other is not fair. No one's underlying needs get addressed. So the ways this couple deals with issues must emphasize a fair process leading to a fair outcome. Because they keep struggling over what's fair, the dog/duck couple keep veering away from discussing their real issues. If they were a car, their greatest need would be for a steering wheel.

It's as if every time an issue came up, instead of steering toward a solution, this couple drifted toward talking about how they talk to each other.

The dog says, "It's not fair that you don't stop and listen to my needs and deal with them." The duck says, "It's not fair that you don't make me feel safe in the way you bring up your issues." Since this unfairness leads this type of couple to go in a circle, the steering wheel would be something that brings fairness to both sides and keeps them on course.

Here's the steering wheel. First, acknowledge that the pattern you keep falling into is a disaster and is using up energy you could be spending enjoying each other. Second, instead of blaming each other, split the difference. The duck has to be less skittish, and the dog has to be less confrontational. The dog needs to be heard. So the duck should listen. The duck needs to feel safe. So the dog should be more calm.

In other words, the duck must say, "I'll be happy to listen to your needs and deal with them if you make me feel safe." The dog must say, "I'll be happy to make you feel safe if you listen to my needs and deal with them." Then the couple could steer a nice path down the middle of both their needs.

But both people will have to cooperate in this. You don't have a steering wheel if both people aren't doing what's fair at the same time.

It's fair that they each see the other as having good intentions. It's fair to understand that people aren't perfect. Dogs are going to bark too loud and ducks are going to get skittish. If you start feeling attacked or abandoned whenever this happens, you'll just end up chasing each other around the barn again. If a dog/duck couple finds themselves back in their old pattern, try this. One of you has to say, "Hey, wait a minute. We're doing it again—you know, the dog/duck stuff that gets us nowhere. If you stop being so confrontational, I'll really listen and work this out with you." Or, "If you'll deal with this issue with me, I promise to listen and be patient."

Soon the dog will stop being so confrontational. Soon the duck will stop making such a big deal about the dog's style. This is the point at which the dog/duck couple can really turn things around in their relationship and get closer to the mutual honesty they both believe in.

Because it's so targeted to the dog/duck couple, steering a middle course between barking too loudly and acting too skittish may be the only tool you need to prevent those fights that occur over and over in your relationship. What a time-saver!

CREATING
ABUNDANT
LOVE

Chapter Seven

ONE TRUE CONNECTION A DAY

Most weekend-marriage couples say, "We miss being close and having fun together, but don't we have to stop being irritated by each other before we can do that?" It's a classic chicken-or-egg problem. Which comes first, enjoying each other or solving the problems that prevent you from enjoying each other?

Successful weekend-marriage couples understand that if you wait to feel good about each other before you start enjoying each other, you could wait forever. There's too much irritation built in to the weekend marriage, too little time to solve problems. So successful weekend-marriage couples have uncovered a variety of secrets for how we can bring the love back even in the midst of the time-starved, sometimes irritating lives we lead.

The next few chapters will show you exactly how to make this happen.

When you're living the weekend marriage, the most common

feeling is disconnection. *Where's the love?* you wonder. *I know we love each other. We say it to each other a lot. But when I'm really honest with myself, I wonder how much more there is to our love beyond saying these words. When do we really feel love?*

This is a daunting question. How do you make love happen when you feel disconnected from each other?

INSIGHT FOR ACTION

Your love is there. You just have to make time for each other. It's having some time together, and the intimate loving things you do with that time, that create the sense of abundant love. If it's time where you truly connect, you don't need a lot of it.

I especially remember one workshop I led for weekend-marriage couples. I have to confess that these workshops were as much to help me learn as to help the couples. I had a head full of raw ideas and I put them all out there to see what would take.

At the end of this particular workshop, I was surprised to learn that one of the ideas people found most useful was *Make one true connection a day.* This was surprising to me because I was talking about something so small, so simple, that it might be almost invisible. It's the elementary particle of love. It's a moment. Maybe only a few seconds.

But for that incredibly brief period of time, you and your spouse connect as two people who love each other. As if you were the only two people in the world. It could be something as basic as looking each other in the eyes. It could be a smile. Or an exchange of words. Or a hug. Or a kiss.

It just has to feel like a true connection to both of you, some-thing that cuts deeper, feels more personal than your routine in-teractions. Couples can easily smile, hug, and kiss in the most perfunctory way. And that's okay. It's a great way to signal *We still love each other and we're not mad at each other.*

But a true connection is not perfunctory. You feel you've de-liberately done something to create a little bubble in time and for a moment float away in it. You could make love every night, but a sudden warm hug in the kitchen could make you feel more truly connected.

And you need to do this *every day.* Listen, if there were some medical procedure you needed to do every single day to keep yourself alive, like giving yourself an injection of insulin, you would damned well do it. So why wouldn't you have one true connection every day? It's just as important for the health of your relationship.

Don't let my talk of *one true connection* make you think I'm talking about anything difficult. Less is more. One true connec-tion is usually easier and takes less time than a lot of forced and ir-ritated interactions. The idea is basically that you're cutting through the momentum and routine of your lives to really con-nect. For example, maybe you kiss good-bye every morning. It's nice though it's rushed and perfunctory. But one morning you slow it down. The kiss is longer and deeper. After you kiss, you maintain eye contact. I'm just talking about maybe forty-five sec-onds here. But that's enough to clearly make a true connection.

Here's another example. Couples always ask each other, "How was your day?" That's a nice thing to do. But what if one day dur-ing the first quiet moment in the evening, one of you went up to the other and said, "How have you been feeling these days?" and stood there quietly waiting for a real answer? Showing interest in your spouse like this makes a true connection.

It doesn't have to be particularly deep. One night after you both get home, and after you've done all the little chores you always do like going through the mail, you could sit down in the living room for a few minutes and just catch each other up on what you've been doing.

It doesn't even require talking. Maybe you're sitting watching TV together and one of you starts rubbing the other's feet.

It doesn't have to be one intense moment. You could go for a walk after dinner and feel that the whole experience was comfortable and made you feel close.

It could be creating an opportunity for being supportive. Let's say one of you had been mentioning plans for making a transition at work. You might say, "Let's sit down so you can tell me about your plans and maybe I can offer some suggestions."

It could be that all you'll have time for is getting into bed, except that before you go to sleep you'll lie facing each other, looking into each other's eyes, and saying, "You know, I really love you."

It could be *anything*. But it can't be the same old same old. It can't be sitting together just watching TV—this can be comfortable and relaxing, but you're not really having a true connection with each other. You're having fun separately, except that you're doing so in each other's presence. It can't be having a conversation about whether you can afford to have the bathroom remodeled or about whether you think your youngest kid might have a learning disability.

It could be anything as long as it's the kind of thing you'd do if you were dating and wanted to keep on dating each other.

Here's what couples tell me who make sure they always have one special, positive interaction every day: "It makes me feel safe." They're absolutely right. Since you come together because of love, every day that goes by without experiences of love will make you feel unsafe, because the question gets raised more and more strongly: "Why are we together in the first place?" But if you simply share a kiss that feels like a real kiss, you remember why you're together.

Couples get into trouble because the blunt truth is that you never *have* to truly connect with each other. As long as all your interactions are polite, no one spying on you would ever know the difference. But I've got to tell you the news I've brought back from couples who figured out how to make their love thrive while living the weekend marriage: they've understood that, *Toto, we're not in Kansas anymore. It's no longer business as usual. We'll end up in trouble if we keep thinking we can live our relationship as if we have all the time in the world, as if we can put off really connecting until we have some chance encounter in the future.*

Here's the thing: every day that goes by without making some small but true connection makes it harder to connect like that in the future. These tiny daily connections are the lifeline of your love.

I'd like the chance to prove to you that you have time to do this. National survey data show that, yes, we're incredibly busy, but it's also still possible for anyone to find time to make one true connection a day.

Let's start with the fact that we're all endowed with 168 hours in a week. Now the data show that while everyone is different, the most common pattern when both spouses work is for them to be on the job 45 hours a week, if you factor in all the extras we do for work. Add in about an hour of commuting time each day. Assume people get 7 hours of sleep a night. When you add together all the time people spend working, commuting, and sleeping and then subtract it from 168, this leaves about 69 hours a week. (Trust me, I double-checked the math.)

But it's not, as you know, 69 hours a week of free time. For one thing, there are chores to do. According to the Bureau of Labor Statistics, working women spend about 31 hours a week working around the house, working men spend about 19 hours a week. These numbers seem awfully high to me (although maybe this just reflects on my own slapdash approach to housework). To be conservative, let's call it 15 hours per week for housework. This leaves 54 hours a week.

Then there are social obligations to fulfill, phone calls to make, TV shows to watch. According to media studies, people spend about 28 hours a week watching TV. Let's cut that down to 20 for a busy working couple. This leaves 34 hours. Then people spend about 6 hours a week with friends and relatives, and another 3 hours exercising. This leaves 25 hours a week.

But most people spend one hour a day on grooming. At least one more hour a day is spent preparing food and eating. That's a total of 14 hours a week. This leaves 11 hours. That works out to roughly an hour and a half a day of free time.

We still haven't taken kids into account. According to research out of the University of Maryland, women spend about 6 hours a day with their kids, and men spend about 4 hours a day. But time spent taking care of the kids is usually taken away from things like watching TV and getting together with other people.

So even with kids in the picture and both spouses working outside the home, let's say there's still a half hour to an hour a day available to you as a couple. Granted, that's not a lot of time when you're starting out with 168 hours. Granted, the pace and pressure of our lives is fearsome these days. Granted, it's all too easy to fritter away the little time we have left. *But the time is still available for one true connection a day.*

People always ask me if there were any surprising findings in my research. Here's one that definitely surprised me. Fifteen to thirty minutes a day during the week actually doing things that are part of having a real relationship—not as co-parents, not as roommates, not as business partners, but as people who love each other and show their love—is enough time to maintain that true love connection. But you have to make it happen every day.

A CHALLENGE COUPLES face is that different people need different things in order to make that one true connection each day. That's because different people need different things in order to feel close. You might need physical contact to start feeling close. Or you might need for there to be a period of time without feeling angry with each other. Or you might need to talk about some of the things you've had on your mind. Or you might need to hear your spouse talk about his or her feelings. Even if you don't have a lot of time, you need to spend the time you have doing this kind of thing if you're going to feel close to each other.

What you need in order to start feeling close adds up to your closeness style. What your spouse needs adds up to his closeness style. Adding your needs together gives you your closeness style as a couple. *For you to feel close as a couple, you need to do what works for both of you to get close.*

Knowing this gives you a shortcut to intimacy. It's a mistake to think that it takes a lot of time to get close, even in the midst of your pressure-packed week. Just the way you can feel well dressed quickly if the clothes in your closet all reflect your fashion sense, you can get close quickly if the ways you have of getting intimate reflect your closeness style.

Guerrilla tactics. So invest a bit of your precious time in finding out what you and your spouse need in order to feel close to each other. Here's an exercise you can do when you have a few spare moments. Write down a couple of things that make you feel the two of you are getting close, and have your partner do the same thing. I'm talking about things like, "I start feeling close to you when you stop talking about all the stuff that happened to you during the day and start talking about how you really feel about whatever's important to you." Or, "I feel close when we can just lie in each other's arms without saying anything." Whatever it is that makes you or your partner feel close.

It's nice to have it down on paper, because the other person can hold on to that paper. No forgetting. No misunderstanding. It's like a little personal recipe for love. But if you don't like to write, don't. Whether you write it down or not, the important thing here is that you share this crucial information and then follow through.

Be prepared to hear something surprising. Why not? It's the very nature of the weekend marriage to blind you to what will make your spouse feel close these days. Often what makes weekend-marriage couples feel most loved is something that may not seem to have much to do with the direct expression of affection. One woman, for example, said to her husband, "If you really want me to feel loved, you'll lose twenty-five pounds. Your big old belly says 'I don't love you' to me. All I do is worry about your dropping dead of a heart attack. And I don't feel attracted to you at your current weight."

When we hear something like this, we sometimes find it hard to let it in. Our instinctive response is, *Oh you don't mean it.* My advice to you is to trust what your spouse says. And then show your love in the way she says really means something to her.

A warning. When the two of you sit down and tell each other what will truly make you feel close, this is a sacred ceremony. That's because once you've shared what makes you feel loved, neither of you can plead ignorance anymore. If you say what makes you feel loved and your spouse doesn't do anything about it, you'll feel betrayed. So will your spouse.

But this is also a moment of tremendous opportunity. The way coldness breeds coldness in a relationship, love breeds love. You're too busy to do anything but those specific, targeted things that most make your spouse feel loved. But if you do them, one person's loving actions motivate the other to do loving things. Just like when you were first together.

When people in a relationship know what they need to feel close as well as what their spouse needs, then they've created powerful recipes they can use any time they want for making a true connection quickly.

People make a big deal about what they need to feel close because too often they don't experience much closeness, particularly in the weekend marriage. This makes their spouse feel that getting close to them is complicated. But it's not as hard as you might think. Here's a cool fact I've learned about how people work. If you just *try* to give each other what you both need to feel close, you'll both feel so grateful for the effort that you will feel close.

You have to make sure that you *do* those things that you know make your partner feel close to you. The more ways each of you know, the more likely it is that you'll have a true connection every day.

Here's a mistake people make. They do things with their spouse that would make them feel close, not things that make their spouse feel close. It would be like my cooking lasagna for you because I love lasagna, not because I know you love it.

Jessica made this mistake. She feels close to Todd when she shares her hopes for the future with him. But Todd hears her hopes as demands that he make more money or as difficult problems Jessica's dumping in his lap. She's basically feeding lasagna to a guy who doesn't like lasagna and then wondering why they don't feel close. But if she were to use this guerrilla tactic, she'd know what made Todd feel close to her and do that. For example, if she knows that Todd needs physical contact to start feeling close to her, then she'd be smart to put her arms around him or cuddle up next to him. *She* might not feel all that close when she starts doing it, but the way it works is that when *he* starts feeling closer to her, he'll melt and soften and do things that will make her start feeling closer to him.

It's important to take turns. The next evening it can be Todd's turn to start. He knows Jessica needs him to talk about his hopes for their future. So he does that and then she melts and softens.

Another mistake people make is doing things that used to make you feel close, not doing things that make you feel close now as the people you are now. After all, people and relationships change. In a way, every couple is really two couples at the same time. You're the couple you were when you were first going out together and had more free time. And you're the couple you are now, with each of you feeling so much under the gun.

Hal and Wendy were like this. They started dating when Wendy was in her last year of college. Hal had been working in his father's electrical contracting business since he'd graduated from college, but he was just doing that until he figured out what he really wanted to do. He didn't take the work seriously or put much effort into it. To Wendy, he seemed like a sweet, goofy kid, a little wild but a lot of fun. To Hal, Wendy was the nicest, happiest, most innocent person he'd ever known.

For Hal and Wendy, as for the rest of us, who they were when they were first going out is still an important part of who they are now. That was who they chose to spend their life with. When spouses really think they know each other, this is the part they know and love best.

But there's another Hal and Wendy nine years into their marriage, both working, with two kids. This is the Hal and Wendy who respond in a certain way to the pressures of the weekend marriage. When he's under the gun, sweet, goofy, fun-loving Hal turns into a dictator. He thinks he knows all the answers. He's got to call all the shots. When she's under the gun, Wendy changes from being the most approachable person in the world to being the ice princess. When there's a lot to do, Wendy's always saying, "Don't talk to me, don't touch me, don't bother me."

Now when you tell Hal and Wendy to do loving things for each other because that's what their relationship desperately needs, which "each other" are you talking about? The old Hal and Wendy or the weekend-marriage Hal and Wendy? Left to their own devices, they'll choose the old Hal and Wendy because *they don't know* the new Hal and Wendy. I know that sounds crazy—Hal and Wendy have been living the weekend marriage for years. What's new about it?

But Wendy can't bring herself to believe that bossy Hal is the real Hal. He's just some creep who's kidnapped her Hal and taken over his body. And Hal doesn't know who the heck this cold, aloof Wendy is. She's sure not his sweet old Wendy.

So when Hal and Wendy think of doing things to get close to each other, they instinctively fall back on thinking in terms of the old Hal and Wendy. The old Wendy loved it when Hal came up and took her in his arms. The old Hal loved it when he was doing something and Wendy started goofing around with him. But the new Hal and Wendy hate stuff like this.

It's great news that below the surface our old selves are still there. This means that when we have time to relax and enjoy each other and let go of the cares of the day, who we were when we were first together can rise up out of the ashes and continue the love affair.

But as we live the day to day of our weekend marriage, it's our new selves that we need to make feel loved.

INSIGHT FOR ACTION
Your spouse doesn't feel loved when you do something that *used* to make him feel loved. He doesn't feel loved when you do something that *should* make him feel loved. He feels loved only when you do the kind of thing that makes him feel loved as he is right now.

Whenever a couple starts working with me, one of the first things I do is ask each of them what they think makes the other feel loved. I'm constantly amazed. This is an area where even people who've been married for a long time just don't know each other very well.

The guy will say something like, "She really likes it when I bring her flowers." The woman will look at me as if to suggest, See what I have to deal with? and then she'll say something like, "Flowers are nice but they're no big deal. You want to show me you love me? Then do something about how you always start bugging me the minute you see me in the evening. You have questions for me and things to say to me. You know what would really make me feel loved? If you just left me the hell alone for a while. I need to take care of myself. People have been talking to me all day. I need some quiet."

When it's the woman's turn, she'll say something like, "I know he feels loved when I make him a nice meal." The guy will say something like, "Haven't I told you a million times I don't care about that. I know once I made a big deal about your cooking when we were first dating, but that was because my previous girlfriend had never cooked. So maybe it's all my fault. But what would make me feel loved is if you spent some time with me rather than rushing around the kitchen. I always eat lunch out. I get a good meal every day. I'd be happy eating cereal for dinner if you were just in a good frame of mind and had something to give me."

Statements like these are always a revelation for our spouses. We make a big deal about mutual honesty, but then we spend our time complaining instead of talking about what we most need to be honest about, which is what will most make us feel close and loved. But if you know what makes your spouse feel loved and your spouse knows what makes you feel loved, it's like you've been handed the keys to heaven on earth.

Chapter Eight

ABUNDANT SEX IN A TIME-STARVED WORLD

Just in case you've forgotten how to do it, when two people love each other, they start hugging and kissing and then . . .

But of course you haven't forgotten how to do it. It just can seem that way when you're living the weekend marriage. For many weekend-marriage couples, sex is the first thing to go. It's not that there's literally no time; it's that you can never find enough time that feels right.

Dan and Millie had gone deep into the time-starved lifestyle. He was a software engineer. She juggled taking care of their kids with working as a pediatrician three days a week. Between the two of them, long workdays, meetings scheduled for ungodly hours, and business travel all took their toll. Net result? Dan and Millie had one of those brief conversations I've heard so often:

"When was the last time we made love?"

"God, it was . . . wasn't it last week?"

"You mean Saturday, right? No, because—"

"Oh yeah. I remember, we were going to and then . . . But if it wasn't Saturday, when was it?"

There was a pause. "Honey, it's been a long time."

And they just looked at each other.

Every weekend-marriage couple realizes the same thing at some point: *We're just not making love much anymore.*

Weekend-marriage couples treat making love like something you can postpone. But it isn't.

You can postpone visiting Florence. But suppose you treat making love like that: *So what if we make love this week or next week or . . .* Then it hits you. As Millie put it in a couples session, "You know, life is short. How many opportunities are there to make love? If you miss one of those opportunities, you think you're going to make it up, but you don't. It's just gone." Millie turned from me to Dan. "I'm afraid I'm going to wake up one day an old lady and get really sad thinking about all the times we could've made love and didn't."

Dan tried to make everything better. "But come on, you know, we're so tired. And we don't want to be rushed. And sometimes we're irritable, right? And sometimes, it's like we've been distant, just because of our lives, and it seems so hard to suddenly turn on the sexual connection."

They both sighed. At least they weren't blaming each other.

Blame it on the weekend marriage. But it's not just the lack of time. It's also the fact that the tone of our lives is incredibly antiromantic. Classic weekend-marriage phrases like *"Hey, did you remember to . . . ?"* or *"When are you going to get around to . . . ?"* would cause even teenagers to lose interest in sex.

Sex, like a thunderstorm, emerges naturally out of a couple's romantic atmosphere. When you're horny and in love and obsessed with exploring each other, everything you do contributes to a sexy atmosphere. The way you hug when you greet each other can make it perfectly clear that later on you're going to make love.

But there's a kind of businesslike, let's-just-get-through-everything-we-have-to-do atmosphere in the weekend marriage that can make you feel you'll get whiplash if you make a sexual overture. So you get couples in the situation where they're both basically saying, *I'll do something sexy if you do something sexy first,* but no one makes the first move.

Enough of the gloom. We know what we're up against. But what successful weekend-marriage couples discover is that it doesn't have to be this way. Here are some recipes that work to bring more desire and more sexy, satisfying, romantic lovemaking into your weekend marriage. But for these recipes to work, you have to work the recipes.

Create a charged sexual atmosphere. Feeling sexy toward each other can't emerge out of the clear blue sky anymore than lightning can. Lightning emerges from dark thunder clouds. Usually before you see lightning and hear thunder, you're aware that the atmosphere's changed. Maybe you can smell the ozone. Maybe the air was very still and heavy and suddenly a wind springs up. Maybe the sky gets dark. You expect the lightning before it comes, so that the lightning almost seems like the fulfillment of your expectations.

You can do the same when it comes to sex. I've found that successful weekend-marriage couples do things to create a charged sexual atmosphere.

It doesn't require you to talk about sex directly. It's usually much more of a seductive, suggestive, teasing way of talking, even when the topic is something as mundane as what time you're going to get home from work. The key is that it not be flat and businesslike. Even if sex never directly comes into it, you're talking to each other as if you've just made love or as if you know you're just about to make love.

Another way to create this charged sexual atmosphere is through how you touch each other. Grabbing is out. What's in is touching each other as if one of you were trying to seduce the other. It's indirect, teasing. It can start and then stop. And then start again. One couple talked about how they'd be watching TV and he'd be holding her hand and then very slowly work his way up her arm to her shoulder and neck. She'd feel teased and distracted away from TV and toward lovemaking.

Of course this charged atmosphere doesn't always have to lead to sex. Maybe it won't most of the time. But it will still lead to your making love more often and to your feeling sexier and more romantic when you do make love.

When it comes to sex, fast food can be good food. How can you have a sexual relationship when you don't have much time? Let me use an analogy. A lot of fast food is bad food, but it doesn't have to be. There can be good fast food, too. Think about what fast food is. It's just food when you don't have much time to cook or eat. A hunk of nicely aged cheddar and a juicy peach is fast food. A bag of nuts and dried fruit is fast food. Popping open a plastic container filled with salad stuff is fast food.

Well, it works the same way when it comes to sex. Quickies are the fast food of sex. But they've given a bad name to the idea of being intimate when you don't have much time. Let's face it, a quickie too often refers to a situation where a woman throws some fast action her man's way out of pity for his horniness. He gets a release; she often doesn't. But even if a woman has a relatively short fuse, and a quickie leads to orgasm for both of them, a steady diet of quickie sex won't be truly satisfying for either.

We need to change what it means to have a quickie. Sex without intimacy is like junky fast food. Sometimes it's just what you want, but in the long run a steady diet of it leaves you feeling hollow and more distant than ever. But *real sensual intimacy* can be like great fast food. It doesn't have to take much time and it can be deeply nourishing. What's more, intimacy without sex today creates an atmosphere that perfectly sets the stage for intimacy *with* sex tomorrow.

There are lots of ways to create tiny but true moments of intimacy in a relationship. What's valuable about them is that they can keep the romantic embers lit during the week so that during the weekend it's not such a daunting task to fan the flames of passion.

Here are some suggestions for what you can do to sprinkle sexy, romantic, intimate encounters throughout your brief, rushed time together. I'm offering these suggestions to stimulate you to come up with your own ideas.

- *Take a bath or shower together.* Hey, you got to get clean anyway, right? Why take separate showers when you can take a shower together? I'm not necessarily talking about a long scene from a soft porn movie. Even if it's just a quick shower and all you do is wash each other's backs, it's way more sexy than not doing it.
- *Spend a few minutes massaging your spouse's neck, feet, hands.* The nice thing about this is that you can do it when you're talking

about something or when you're relaxing and listening to music. Take turns.

- *Slow dance.* Maybe the radio's on or maybe you're listening to music on your stereo. It's just as easy to slow dance as it is to sit there. But it's much more intimate.
- *Make out.* Remember making out? It was hot and it was fun. When you're sitting on the couch or standing in the kitchen, why not start to kiss and hug and so on. Don't worry about starting something you don't have time to finish. The point is to do something that's good in itself and creates a sexy atmosphere. You don't need the classic setting, like the backseat of an old Chevy. And if you spend a long time kissing good-bye in the morning, guess what? You've just made out.

The key is to make things like this happen. Remember in high school when you had to take a risk and talk to someone you had your eye on whom you'd never talked to before? You just had to do it. It's the same with the little things we do to create intimate moments.

Nothing beats a long, leisurely meal. If you're eating a lot of fast food, it's really important for your body and soul in incalculable ways now and then to have a nice, leisurely meal. Yes, don't worry, I'm still talking about sex. A hundred brief moments of true intimacy set the stage for a full-blown romantic encounter but they don't substitute for it.

But here's the key to this. You know darned well that the opportunity for prolonged lovemaking almost never appears by itself when you live the weekend marriage. So you have to create these opportunities. Setting them up might in itself be unromantic: "You know, Saturday night we don't have anything planned. And Matt has been clamoring to have a sleepover at Jeff's house. If we let Matt sleep over at Jeff's and bring Bridget to my mother's house, we can have a romantic Saturday night in this house to ourselves. What do you think, do you want to set it up?"

Successful weekend-marriage couples tell me that you can't worry about the initial awkwardness of planned opportunities for lovemaking. It can feel a little uncomfortable at first, more like a decision than a feeling. But understand what you're doing. This is really an exercise in planned spontaneity. It's true that you had to set up the time and place. But everything else that happens can be spontaneous.

Remember why they invented appetizers. (Don't worry. I'm *still* talking about sex.) When I was a kid I never got the idea of appetizers. My mother would always yell at me that if I ate a slice of bread, I'd spoil my appetite for dinner. But then I'd see grown-ups stuffing their faces with snacks before dinner. They made it acceptable by calling them *appetizers.* But still—eating to make yourself hungry???

But now I understand. You're busy. You're running around. You're not in a food frame of mind. The thought of suddenly having a big old plate of food shoved under your face isn't, well, appetizing. But they seduce you with a little tiny plate with a couple of cute nothings on it. And that gets your juices going so you're ready to face the meal with gusto.

I'm here to tell you that it works the same way when it comes to making love for weekend-marriage couples. You may have sexual hunger, but it's deeply buried below layers of irritability and fatigue. So what do you do if in the midst of a busy weekend you suddenly find an hour and a half of free time dropped in your laps? How do you generate a sexual spark when you haven't had time to stoke the romantic fires between you?

The question really is, how do you have sex when you don't feel sexy?

The first thing you have to do is accept a reality that all successful weekend-marriage couples accept. If you wait to feel sexy before you start doing sexy things, you may never have sex again. Scared you, didn't I?

Let's say that good fortune suddenly offers you the time, the place, and the opportunity for making love. Now here's how it will work for you when you're a successful weekend-marriage couple. At first you don't feel sexy. Why would you? You've been spending your time catching up on paperwork. In the past you would've dealt with this by saying, *Well, I don't feel sexy so I can't possibly start anything.* Instead you should think of it like singing songs around a campfire. Okay, maybe the wood is green and damp. Maybe it will take a long time before a fire gets going. So do you sit there and say that the rule is you can't sing campfire songs until the campfire is roaring? No. You start singing, even though you may not totally feel like it, even though there is no campfire yet. This encourages you to light the fire and gets you going for when the fire's lit!

It's the same when it comes to sex. Of course it feels awkward to start making out when you don't feel sexy. But successful weekend-marriage couples understand that you'll never get it going if you don't get going. So even though they're not feeling particularly sexy, they start the process. They just remember to be patient with themselves and each other.

It's a mistake to think that the more distant you've been, the harder it is to get going. The right way to think of it is that the more distant you've been, the more important it is to keep going. With a little encouragement, nature will take its course and your love for each other will do the rest.

Now here's what some successful weekend-marriage couples have found. You can't get too invested in a particular outcome. That hour and a half you thought was more than enough time for a satisfying session of lovemaking may take you on a surprising journey. Maybe you started off with physical sensuality but when you started feeling comfortable and connected to each other, you started talking. Maybe instead of having sex you end up having a nice conversation.

Failure or success? Obviously a failure if your goal was sexual intercourse. But there are all kinds of intercourse. Maybe the two of you needed emotional and verbal intercourse to build a much-needed bridge. Maybe this bridge will make lovemaking more likely next time.

INSIGHT FOR ACTION

It's important to think of any attempt either of you make to get close as a success. Any way you actually do get close when you live the weekend marriage is a huge success. Celebrating these successes helps create the atmosphere that makes intimacy flow more easily.

Here's a **guerrilla tactic.** The next time you're thinking of making love, don't. Instead invest a little time in talking to each other about what you like and what you don't like when it comes to making love:

Tell each other "What I most wish you understood about my sexuality is . . ."

Tell each other what you'd like more of and what you'd like less of in sex.

And tell each other what you need the other to do so you feel desired.

It's really important when you do this not to offer critical comments about what you're hearing. I know that's hard to do if your partner tells you that one of the things that makes him feel desired is if you tousle his hair and talk baby talk to him. But you won't have to act on everything you're told.

This information is crucial for weekend-marriage couples. Not having time changes things. If you had a week in Paris, you could afford to roam around aimlessly. But if you had only a day or two in Paris, you'd want to make sure you'd figured out what you wanted to see in advance so you could guarantee you hit the high spots. It's the same when it comes to lovemaking. The less time you have, the more important it is to understand and respect each other's sexuality. And to do that, you need answers to these questions.

Here's another **guerrilla tactic.** As you're well aware, unless you're somehow perfectly compatible sexually, there are real differences in what each of you likes during lovemaking. These can be differences in pacing. In who does what to whom. You name it. When couples have time, they try to meet both people's needs. Or at least compromise. But when you live the weekend marriage, here's what you do.

Find a flat stone or an old poker chip or some big foreign coin.

Write the letters LML on it. These letters stand for *let's make love.* One of you holds the stone first and whenever he or she wants to make love, the stone gets handed over. That's it. Unless there's a really good reason, you have to make love then. But now the other person has the stone and next time they can cash it in when they want to make love.

You can take this further. You might decide that whoever holds the LML stone not only gets to say when you make love, but gets to be in charge of what happens when you make love. If you want, you can think of this as *taking turns being each other's sex slave.* Now before you freak out, of course I don't mean that anyone is literally anyone's slave. And of course *no one should ever do anything sexually that he or she feels uncomfortable doing.*

But what's great about this technique is that each time you make love, at least one person is guaranteed to have it go just the way he or she wants. The other person is guaranteed to have a sense of giving satisfaction. And as you take turns, you learn a lot about each other's sexuality. It's a win/win/win solution.

Here's how to take turns being each other's sex slave. When it's your turn, you decide who does what in bed, when, to whom, and in what way. It's your turn to be the writer, director, and star of that sexual encounter. It's your turn to get what you want the way you want it. Unless it crosses some line, your spouse has to do what you want.

Don't make the mistake of thinking that because it's your turn you have to act like a lion tamer constantly barking directions. Remember: you're in complete charge as long as what you're doing is focused on your needs. Now your need might be not to have to talk and for your spouse to lead. Accept whatever it is you really feel and want. After all, you don't have time to do anything else.

But remember that you're taking turns. The next time, it's your spouse's turn to initiate lovemaking and have it go however he or she wants. Then you keep on taking turns.

Over time, it will all balance out. Each person's needs will get met. Maybe not each and every time. There's no time for that in the weekend marriage. But each and every time *someone's* needs will get met.

Chapter Nine

WHO CAN MAKE MORE GOOD THINGS HAPPEN?

"More of the good stuff—that's what my husband and I need to get us through these busy days." This is what one woman said who was living a successful weekend marriage. We *all* want more of the good stuff. Couples often tell me that one of the worst things about the weekend marriage is that it feels like a relationship desert. The two of you can go on and on for days without any of the good things happening that make love feel like love. And you need as many of them as possible. I'm not talking about deep moments of intimacy. I'm talking about *anything*—even just a single word of affection.

Jamie and Chuck were like a lot of weekend-marriage couples. The disagreements and resentments had built up, but because they were so starved for time, they never seemed able to resolve their problems once and for all. For example, there was Jamie's mother. Jamie agreed with Chuck—her mom was annoying. But she was sick of hearing Chuck complain about her. And she was unwilling to push her mother out of their lives as much as Chuck wanted.

Then there was the issue of saving money. Jamie had grown up poor and wanted to save every penny they could for their retirement. Chuck had the attitude, *Things will take care of themselves.* Jamie was always on Chuck's back about his spending too much money.

And there were plenty of other sources of irritation.

Now let's add time to the picture. Or lack of time, I should say. A conflict would arise. There wouldn't be time to talk it through. Jamie and Chuck would be left with their anger at each other. This was particularly true since, feeling under pressure, they'd say things to each other more intensely than they needed to just to drive home their points faster.

Now, when you have a fight with your spouse and the anger reaches a certain level, it takes a specific chunk of time for the two of you to make peace and get close again. Let's say for the sake of argument that making up takes three hours. If you're in the middle of a long weekend, you can take those three hours in one chunk, and voilà, you've made up. But when you're living the weekend marriage, you might have only twenty minutes per day together. At that rate, it could take *nine days* to make peace and get close.

And that changes things. Put your relationship in the refrigerator for nine days and it starts feeling like a cold dead thing. You wouldn't put your cat in the fridge for nine days!

So you can't wait for the natural processes to heal things when you're in the midst of the time-starved lifestyle. Let's say Jamie and Chuck worked out their differences over money and mothers. That's fine, but it doesn't bring them back to love. It just brings them back to not being angry at each other. It's the good things that happen between you, not your resolving your differences, that are the lifeblood of marriage. I mean *actually doing specific loving things that make you feel your relationship is filled with love.*

You may think this isn't possible when you're mad at each other. Not hurling-insults mad, but even just keeping-your-distance mad.

But you're wrong. I know you *can* do that because I've seen it time and time again. You know there've been times when you were mad at each other and you got together with another couple, for example. You didn't want that couple to see you not getting along so you acted nice to each other, and the next thing you knew you were feeling way better about each other. At the end of the evening you were saying, "Wow, we have to go out with Sam and Meg more often." But Sam and Meg didn't bring any special mojo. You did it yourselves.

And you have to do it. Wouldn't it be nuts to say that you have to be completely healthy before you start eating healthful food? Well, it's just as nuts to say that you have to solve all your problems and be feeling good about each other before you can have positive experiences with each other. Eating healthful food is good for you even if you don't feel like eating it or you aren't feeling particularly healthy. It's doing loving things that does the most to promote the health of your relationship, *especially* when you're not feeling good about each other.

But couples who are struggling in the weekend marriage tend to make a fatal mistake. They think they have to solve their problems before they can do loving things. I understand where they're coming from. Who wants to make nice when you feel angry or deprived? But here's the thing. There are always unresolved bubbles of anger in our weekend marriages. But we just don't have the time to solve every single problem in our relationship. So if you waited until you felt all perfect and lovey-dovey, you could end up never doing loving things.

You see the danger.

But there's also a wonderful opportunity here.

A truly revolutionary idea emerged in my research into the weekend marriage. I kept seeing something amazing.

INSIGHT FOR ACTION

Couples didn't thrive because they did nothing but work on their problems until they were all solved. Couples thrived because in the little time they had they had fun together, they were affectionate, and they got close in spite of whatever problems were simmering. And you're able to make this happen, too, in spite of the fact that you may be mad at each other. The more mad you are, the more important it is that you make it happen, just the way the sicker you are, the more important it is that you take in healthful nourishment.

Of course the question is how to make good things happen in spite of the fact that you're too busy or too pissed off to be in the mood for it.

Here's what you're up against. I call it the standoff. Anyone who's been in a long-term relationship will recognize it. Let's say that as you were getting ready to go to work, your spouse spoke disrespectfully to you. Maybe he called you an idiot, an airhead. And that really hurt. But the truth is that you'd promised to pick up the dry cleaning yesterday and then forgot it. None of his really good shirts were clean and he had an important meeting that he'd told you about. So you had a fight. You're mad at each other. He feels frustrated. You feel hurt.

The standoff is when you're waiting for each other to make the first move to reconcile and get close. You know that you did something wrong, but you're convinced that what your spouse did was even worse. You both might want to say "I'm sorry," but you just want the other to say it first.

Now, of course, standoffs resolve themselves every day. Some mysterious melting happens and you or your spouse makes that all-important first move. But when you're living the weekend marriage, you can't wait for mysterious currents to carry you into each other's arms. In fact, because you have so little time together, the standoff can continue for so long that the distance between you congeals like thickening, transparent Jell-O. And so it gets harder and harder to make the first move.

Standoffs are inevitable. You need a force more powerful to prevent them from keeping you apart. And I think that more powerful force is our love of gambling.

So employ this **guerrilla tactic.** Bet your spouse that in the next week you can do more positive, loving, fun, nurturing, affectionate things for him than he can do for you. Bet something significant so that you both really feel motivated to win. Some people bet money. Some people set it up so the loser has to do some chore or give the winner an hour-long, full-body massage.

I'm sure you'll have no trouble thinking of something good to wager. Don't forget to keep score—you could put marks on the calendar, for example.

Now here's the cool part. No matter what happens, *you'll both win*. If you're the one who has to pay off the bet, that means your spouse has done more good things for the relationship than you have. You're still the winner! I can't imagine a better deal.

And I think you should renew this bet every week for the rest of your time-starved lives together. My husband and I do that.

Now I understand an objection some people have to this: that you're making some loving gesture even though you're not in the mood for it. But so what? We do lots of things that are good for us that we're not in the mood to do. I'm rarely in the mood to exercise. I'm never in the mood to get out of bed early in the morning.

The weekend marriage is probably the one part of your life, more than any other, where it's most important to act beyond your moods. That's because negativity is just as contagious as affection. You need to prevent yourselves from falling victim to an emotional Ice Age brought on by the standoff.

Some people feel that their integrity doesn't permit them to be affectionate if they're angry, as if a moment of affection would cancel out what they see as their legitimate anger. But I think this is like saying that you can't eat because you owe five thousand dollars on your credit cards. Okay, you owe money, but you have to eat to keep yourself healthy. Okay, you're angry, but you have to share affection to keep your relationship healthy. And besides, why not show integrity for your hopes for love as much as you do for your feelings of anger?

Besides, all you need to do to win the bet is to make *something* good happen for each other. If you're angry and hurt, you don't have to say "I love you" if at that moment those words would turn to ashes in your mouth. But there are lots of positive, healthful things you can do. For example, if you see that your spouse is particularly tired, maybe you can offer to do something for her that you wouldn't ordinarily do. If you see that he's worried, maybe you could offer some kind of reassurance, or the opportunity to talk about it.

When it comes to doing these positive things for each other, in my experience what people need to appreciate is how far the *little* things go.

I remember one woman telling me that her husband brought her flowers every Friday evening. That was good, but she got really excited when she talked about how every *day* when he came home from work he *lifted her up* and kissed her. She was a petite woman. Lifting her up was no big deal for him. But it was that extra something that added life to a hi-honey-I'm-home kiss that might otherwise have been routine. It was such a little thing. It took no extra time. But it literally lifted her up.

So forget the grand romantic gestures. You don't have time for them anyway. But how much time does it take to stop everything and give your spouse a big hug? How much time does it take to wake up your spouse in the morning by getting back into bed and kissing for a minute? How much time does it take to remember to say "I love you" on the phone.

I'm not going to insult your intelligence by giving you more examples. You have such a wide field to choose from—something nice, something kind, something thoughtful, something affectionate.

Whatever things you do to win the bet can also create more intimacy if you do it right. Intimacy is about seeing through the veil. You're intimate with someone when you see things about each other that other people don't see. So you could win a point, for example, by saying something like "You seem really bummed from your day. Did something bad happen at work?" Doing something to help your spouse feel seen is always good for your relationship but it also makes you feel closer.

And if you're mad, you can still say something like "I know we're mad at each other, but I want you to know I still love you," or "I'm so proud of you."

In the rushed, frazzled, hard-to-connect world of the weekend marriage, the monster dies a little every time you do something positive for each other.

Here's another **guerrilla tactic** that helps end the standoff. Suppose, like so many weekend-marriage couples, that the two of you have gotten to a hurt, distant place. Someone did something, someone said something, you barely remember what, and now you're just mad at each other. You'd like it to stop, but you're both waiting for the other to make the first move.

The guerrilla tactic consists of your making the first move even though it's not fair that you do it, even though you don't feel like doing it. But you do it because you're thinking two, three moves ahead. You know someone's got to do something like this. You know that once the standoff is ended, this is the kind of thing you're going to feel like doing. So why not you? Why not now?

Let's call this breaking the ice. What qualifies? *Anything.* Taking your spouse in your arms. Bringing a gift. Taking your spouse out for a nice meal. Saying something loving or complimentary. Even just agreeing with your spouse when you might've disagreed in the past. It's so easy. And after they do it, everyone always says they wish they'd done it sooner.

Chapter Ten

FINDING TIME IN A TIME-STARVED WORLD

When I first started working on this project, I described it to a woman who lived in my neighborhood. She fit into the classic weekend-marriage mold. Her husband worked long hours; she was a teacher with two kids, plus she had responsibility for her aging parents. In a challenging, actually in a rather bitchy, voice she said to me, "What are you going to do, help people find more time? Listen, I've tried, and it's impossible, so don't even bother."

I totally understood how she felt. How can we possibly find more time? It would be as if you told a friend you were broke and she said, "You must have extra money lying around. Just look for it." How can you be broke and have extra money lying around?

And so who has extra *time* lying around? Besides, don't we often find people who claim they can help us better manage our time to be really annoying? "Give me a break!" one woman said when I was silly enough to talk about her managing her time better. "I'm already multitasking and I hate it. If you really want to help me, show me how I can *waste* some time. That would be a treat."

She was right. Time management is too often about cramming more stuff in. That's great for busy executives, but for weekend-marriage couples, hey, we're crammed enough as it is. We don't want to be shown how we can juggle more balls. We want fewer balls to juggle.

INSIGHT FOR ACTION

What we really need when we're living the weekend marriage is time to waste. Time we can use not to accomplish anything or be productive, but to have fun with the person we love and get close again. You can't find time like this. You have to take it. And you'll take it only if you realize that the health of your relationship is at stake.

So I'm not going to show you how to manage your time more efficiently. But I am going to show you how you can find time to "waste" on your most precious resource: your love.

Don't bother asking anyone to give you some time, because no one has any time to give. Just **take** *the time you need.* This is definitely a **guerrilla tactic,** and if anyone asks me if I've said this, I'm going to deny it. But people, starting with your boss, have a million and one ideas about what you should do with your time. Successful weekend-marriage couples just, well, steal the time they need for each other.

"You know, I really do work hard," Stephanie said. "No one can say that I don't earn every penny I'm paid. And then they treat you like you're in high school. You have only so many sick days—you know the drill. I just decided a while back that I'm going to give myself relationship days every now and then. I think they're more important than sick days. I see people here going through divorces and they can be pretty useless for months. So what if I take a sick day for my relationship? It keeps me and my marriage healthy."

Stephanie is one of a number of people who use guerrilla tactics to find time to waste on love. Sometimes we must be reduced to this. But it's all for a good cause. Think of it like this. We've been taking as sacred all the obligations that use up our time. God forbid that one weekend we should cancel plans to visit a relative or skip some stupid neighborhood event. But what we're really doing is saying that every use of time in our lives is sacred except for our relationship. That's the one thing we sacrifice for everything else.

And that's upside down and backward. You want to talk sacred? Outside of God, nothing's more sacred than love. So maybe stealing time for love is actually your sacred obligation.

Use your appointment book to carve out sacred time for the two of you to be together. Jerry's parents had been married for forty years and they were still going strong. I asked him what their secret was. "I'm not sure," he said. "They may be doing stuff I really don't want to know about. But I'll tell you one thing they did. They had this Thursday-night date night thing when I was growing up. And they never violated it."

We all have commitments in our lives we treat as sacred. Well, in the same way, you should set aside special time to be with each other. Treat that as sacred, too. I've heard so many different ways couples do this. Getting up early on Wednesday and Sunday to make love. The Saturday-night date. The long walk late every Sunday afternoon. The second Friday every month that you take off from work to play hooky together.

Guerrilla tactics. A great thing to do is to make a decision about how much intimacy time per week you're going to have. This is time for just the two of you to get close and enjoy being with each other. It's a quantity of sacred time that can't be violated. You build everything else around it.

Let's say you decide you're going to have seven hours of intimacy time a week come hell or high water. A half an hour per day Monday through Friday. Two hours on Saturday. Two and a half hours on Sunday. Or however you want to do it. The extra time you have is great, but what really creates positive energy is your knowing that you have this time and that nothing and no one can touch it. This will do wonders for morale in your relationship.

Use money to buy time. If you don't have any extra money or you're a low-income wage earner, I apologize for bringing this solution up. I've been poor myself—I know what it's like. Everything is harder. You can't hire someone to do some work for you so you can have time with your spouse. But I'll tell you what I did when I didn't have any money. My kids were little and I traded off with other parents. They'd give me time by babysitting my kids and then I'd give them time by babysitting their kids. The neat part of this is that if you have two little kids the way I did, two more kids isn't really much extra work, and the kids love it.

But lots of people today earn a high enough income so they can at least think about the possibility of hiring other people to help in ways that free up time. Frannie never saw her husband during the week because he worked such long hours, but his weekends were usually free. One summer Frannie had the idea of their using a landscaping service to take over the lawn and gardening chores. Bert balked at this. It was too much money. And in truth they didn't have tons of money to fling around.

Here's the thing, though. In the summer Bert would spend hours mowing, raking, weeding, and so on. Then he'd be tired from all that. And there were always other things to do. Not hiring a landscaping service was preventing Frannie and Bert from doing anything that was fun together. This made Frannie resentful, which bled into the rest of the time they had to be together. In terms of their relationship, the price Bert was paying to save about a hundred and fifty bucks a month was totally not worth it.

This is how to think about using money to buy time. If you spend X amount of dollars to, say, hire a babysitter instead of taking the kids with you when you go out to dinner, what will those dollars buy you in relationship time? Most people end up feeling it's worth it.

Spend less time with time-wasters. Social and family obligations. These words hang like a dead weight around the neck of most relationships. Sometimes it's fun, but a little goes a long way, particularly when you're talking about people who aren't fun.

Jody and Mark once added up all the time they spent in a

month with their mothers and siblings and friends: thirty-eight hours. They couldn't believe it. This was time they didn't always enjoy, time that added stress to their lives, time that took away from their ability to be together just the two of them.

Now of course you're not going to stop seeing everyone. But you do need to put first things first. Placing your relationship on a starvation diet to feed other people who don't need it is nuts. And imagine what a difference it would make if Jody and Mark could take thirty of those thirty-eight hours and give them to themselves. That's an hour a day over the course of a month. This would make a huge difference to their relationship, but it wouldn't make much of a difference to anyone else.

The **guerrilla tactic** here is to do the equivalent of taking the phone off the hook: if someone asks you to do something, tell them you're just not available. Even if you are available. You can't throw away chunks of your precious relationship time just because someone wants to get together with you. I know you can't actually say this to anyone, but your attitude has to be, *We'll get together with* you *once we've had enough time for us.*

Make sure the ways you spend your time are in line with your priorities. Let me tell you the mistake some people make who are struggling with the weekend marriage. They'll do things like spend precious weekend time doing things for the house, but if you ask them what's most important to them, they'll say, "My family." There's something wrong if you care about your family but live for your house. In the same way there's something wrong if your spouse is the love of your life but she gets the leftovers of your time, the way you feed your dog leftovers from the table.

Suppose every evening on your way home from work and every Saturday and Sunday morning you asked yourself, *What's most important to me?* I'm sure that as long as you allocate your time in line with your priorities, you'll have a healthier relationship.

Identify what's important for you to leave undone. The big winners among weekend-marriage couples were those who did less, not more. For them, the two most romantic words in the English language are the *no* they say to others and the *yes* they say to each other. Talk about **guerrilla tactics.** I know that leaving stuff undone means that stuff gets left undone. Sometimes it lies there staring you in the face, like the plot of land that used to be a vegetable garden but now is a scraggly nothing. What will happen in time, though, is that you'll come to see everything you've left undone as a proud reminder of everything you're doing to have abundant love.

Take midweek miniweekends. It sounds like a paradox, but weekend time doesn't have to exclusively take place on the weekend. A very effective **guerrilla tactic** some couples use is to religiously set aside a Wednesday night or a Tuesday lunch as a romantic interlude. For years when our kids were little, because our odd schedules allowed it, my husband and I kept Thursday mornings just for us. It was often the only quality couple time we had.

You might need to experiment with different times of the week to figure out when is best for you to have a midweek miniweekend. But this guerrilla tactic works because for some reason we tend to treat the midweek miniweekend as more sacred than much of our regular weekend time.

Just do it and don't feel guilty. Stacy and Larry were firm believers in cursing the darkness rather than lighting a candle. They'd complain, like most weekend-marriage couples, about the pace of their lives and about how much they "missed" each other. But when I suggested that they just go ahead and take the time they needed, they started making excuses. This involved mostly feeling guilty about saying *no* to bosses, friends, and family members.

What they didn't understand is how we all fall victim to the Rip Van Winkle syndrome. This is the tendency we all have in the midst of our lives to kind of fall asleep and then wake up without first realizing how much time has passed. Of course we don't literally fall asleep. But we get so hypnotized by the speed and routine of our lives, like someone staring at a giant, fast-moving merry-go-round turning and turning endlessly, that we completely lose track of time. It's not true that if you lose time for your relationship this month, you'll make it up next month. If you lose time this month, the Rip Van Winkle syndrome means that you'll fall into a trance and only realize years from now that you've deprived your relationship of the time it needs month after month.

So don't delay doing what's necessary to give your relationship more time. Some of the things you do to grab more time might feel radical to you. They might even make you feel a little uncomfortable. But they'll be the healthiest thing you've done in a long time. And how can you feel guilty about that?

Chapter Eleven

IT'S QUALITY, NOT QUANTITY

Ted watched with growing dismay as his relationship with Molly deteriorated. "We're turning into one of those couples who go into therapy because they bicker all the time," he told his best friend.

Ted was puzzled because he'd actually tried hard to prevent this from happening. When their first child was due, he and Molly decided that she would quit her job as a real-estate broker and stay home to take care of the baby. Ted was earning a good income as a chemical engineer. They figured that there'd been enough pressure on their lives with their both working before the baby came. They knew how much care a baby required. But they believed that with Molly home all day she'd get just enough rest and be enough on top of things so their evenings would have something to look forward to.

It didn't work out that way. Taking care of the baby and the house took more out of Molly than either of them could have predicted. Even though Molly did what she could to have the baby ready for bed by the time Ted got home, so he could enjoy the baby for a few minutes, a pile of chores would have accumulated that still had to be gotten through. And most days the baby turned out to have had a late nap and was awake half the evening.

Ted saw quickly that he had almost no time with Molly when she wasn't completely exhausted. They started the pattern of nagging and bickering that's so common with weekend-marriage couples. This is the monster, of course: two nice people with normal needs who are turned against each other by the stressful demands of their lives. They knew how important it was to be honest with each other, but both felt under so much pressure that neither wanted to hear what the other said.

So Ted had a bright idea. He figured that the problem was that they simply didn't have enough time together. Ted had done what he could to help when he got home. But now his idea was that they would do all the chores together instead of each doing chores separately. They'd fold laundry together. Clean up the kitchen together. Bathe the baby together.

In theory this was an excellent idea: find some way to have more time together. But there was a profound flaw.

When Ted and Molly were first going out, they knew there was something special in their relationship because they had so much fun together. They knew they were both responsible, hardworking people, but this was the vision on which they based their relationship: a lifetime of fun together.

So what in the world made Ted think that now they could feel close by doing things that weren't fun? Life isn't a beer commercial where you can have a grand old time washing a car, laughing while you splash water on each other. Folding laundry is just folding laundry, especially when you're exhausted.

Here's what Ted really "accomplished" with his solution. He spent more time with Molly but the quality of their time together deteriorated. That ended up scaring them even more. They started feeling they were toxic to each other. It's a terrible feeling when you spend most of your time together rubbing each other the wrong way.

Ted and Molly didn't understand something that turns out to be an important secret of success for people who live the weekend marriage. Yes, you do have less time together. But the solution to less time isn't simply more time together. It's not about the quantity of the time you spend together. It's about the quality of the time.

INSIGHT FOR ACTION

People evaluate their relationships based on how *good* the time they spend together is, not on how much time they have together. So it's important to avoid spending time with each other doing things that will most likely annoy or disappoint you. Try to be together mostly in ways that make you feel good about each other and bring you closer.

Guerrilla tactics. One way I think about this insight is to say *maximize quality time and minimize junk time.* People think that because they're so busy and don't have much time together they should try to cram as much any-old-kind-of-time together as they possibly can, as Ted did with Molly. But this means that they end up doing a lot of things that don't enhance their relationship but instead put them in conflict-making situations. So just the way you wouldn't do errands or laundry together on a first date with someone, try not to do anything together that's not fun or intimate or relationship enhancing while you're living the weekend marriage.

This insight flies in the face of what it means to be in a relationship for a lot of people. They have the idea that if you're together, you're together. You try to do as much as you can together, and you evaluate your relationship by how many different things you can do together and still get along. Then when these people find they can't get along with their spouse while doing something—maybe they can't get along cooking together—it makes them sad. They think their relationship is marked as inferior. You can think of this as the Togetherness Theory of Relationships: "Through all kinds of weather,/Even if the sky should fall,/As long as we're together,/It doesn't really matter at all."

I actually subscribed to this theory myself for a long time. Like a lot of people whose parents had a terrible marriage (and also some people whose parents seemed to have a terrific marriage), to me togetherness seemed like the hallmark of relationship success. But then I found that I was subjecting my relationship to a standard that was completely unfair and inappropriate when you're living the weekend marriage.

I know this isn't the greatest analogy, but would you think that you had a great relationship with your cat because you could go everywhere and do everything with your cat? I don't think so. You wouldn't take your cat out dancing, for example. You'd think you had a great relationship with your cat because things were great when you did kitty-type things together, and that's it.

We shouldn't impose inappropriate expectations on our relationship. What happens when we live the weekend marriage is that our time gets filled with things that are completely unconnected to what makes our relationship feel great. Do you think Ted and Molly would've gotten together in the first place if the dating test was what a great time they had with each other folding laundry?

Now I'm aware that this insight can have some radical implications. It might mean that some evenings you spend only ten minutes together in the middle of a stressful, busy week when you're hungry to spend more time with each other. You could find more time to be together, but you know how irritable you are and the time you'd spend together would be taken up getting on each other's nerves while you walked up and down supermarket aisles.

Just think about how you'll feel when you're falling asleep if you put the emphasis on the quality of your time together. Won't you feel better thinking about your spouse if you had no memories from that day of junk time you spent stepping on each other's toes? Maybe you didn't have much time together, but what little time you had was top quality.

You'd better not try to implement this guerrilla tactic without talking it over with your spouse. He or she will just feel abandoned if you suddenly say that you don't want to do chores together anymore. You've got to say something like "You know, yesterday when we did X together, we just got on each other's nerves. I know we thought that spending time together doing X would bring us closer, but let's face it, it didn't and it never has. I'd really rather spend time with you when we can enjoy each other. What do you say about this—from now on, you do X, I'll do Y, and if we have time when we're done, we can go for a walk together or sit down and have a glass of wine."

And if you don't have time to do those things when you finish all the chores, well, I say even no time together is better than time where you get on each other's nerves. Never put your relationship at risk, never create more negative than positive energy, especially in an activity where there's no chance of your getting close and enjoying each other.

This works to strengthen your relationship. If you spend too much junk time together in the weekend marriage, you irritate each other and end up feeling less desire to be together. But if you refuse to be together unless it's good, then your desire to be together will force you to come up with activities where that can really happen. So don't worry about increasing the total amount of time you spend together. Instead focus on improving the quality of the time you do spend together.

To substitute quality time for junk time, it has to be true quality time, based on what's always made it quality time for the two of you. You wouldn't take your colicky baby to your favorite romantic restaurant and say, "Gee, where's the romance?" as your kid was screaming his head off. So in the same way, rule out topics like whether or not you should switch pediatricians or start saving more for your retirement if you want to lie around and have a great conversation with each other.

When I asked people what they did that, for them, made it true quality time, some interesting themes came up:

Sometimes quality time consisted of guilty pleasures. A walk in the park might not seem like a big deal on a Sunday morning. But it might be a renewing experience if you have that same walk in the park after dropping your kid off at soccer practice under a friend's supervision, instead of your having to watch him for the ten thousandth time run up and down the field.

Sometimes quality time consisted of doing things you find romantic. This is very personal. For one person, a bed strewn with rose petals is magic. For another, it's just a mess. For one person, dancing in a room lit with a dozen candles is the height of romance. For another person, it's dark, smoky, and makes him self-conscious about how poorly he dances. It's for you and your partner to decide what's truly romantic.

Sometimes quality time consisted of doing things strongly associated with good memories. "We love to go to Luigi's. It's not the greatest restaurant in the world, but they have these quiet tables in back. And we used to go there when we were just starting out. It always felt romantic. I'm embarrassed to admit this, but part of it is that Luigi's always reminded me of the Italian restaurant where Lady and the Tramp ate spaghetti together and they both started eating that one long strand until their noses touched."

Sometimes quality time consisted of an indulgence. Why is sex often better if you book a nice hotel room just to get away together? There's something about indulging yourselves that drives home the sense that what you're doing is true quality time. It doesn't have to involve spending money. Staying up late together every now and then when you really should be sleeping is also an indulgence.

Sometimes quality time consisted of doing something special.

Let's face it, it can sometimes take work to make special things happen, but it's usually worthwhile. Sometimes, though, a wonderful opportunity will fall in your lap if you just keep your eyes open. Here's an example.

Judy and Pete were in the habit of making love on Friday nights. There's nothing wrong with having something you can count on in your life, especially with the crazy schedules weekend-marriage couples have.

But one Friday night, as they got into bed, for some reason they found themselves talking about what they were like when they first met and some of the things they'd wanted to do in their lives. This led to a conversation about things each wanted to do before they died, adventures they wanted to have (Pete wanted to pilot a boat all the way up the Mississippi as far as he could go, starting in New Orleans), places they wanted to visit (Judy all her life had wanted to visit sub-Saharan Africa, some place really exotic like Zanzibar). It was a wonderful conversation, full of hope and the anticipation of pleasure. At one point, Pete was tempted to start kissing Judy and move them along toward making love. He was glad he resisted the temptation. Before they knew it, they'd spent three and a half hours sharing hopes and dreams. When they realized what time it was, they were too tired to make love. But this was the most intimate they'd been in a long time. Pete was glad he hadn't interrupted that special time.

Chapter Twelve

FINDING LOVE IN YOUR FRANTIC EVENINGS

Let's face it, if a weekend-marriage couple is going to have any time together on a weekday, it's probably going to happen in the evening. Mornings are just too frantic for most of us.

Now if you want to know how we all wish it would go, just watch a rerun of *I Love Lucy*. Ricky walks in the door and says, "Hi honey, I'm home." Lucy runs up to him and says, "Hi honey, how was your day?" Ricky talks about how he's beat. Lucy offers to get him a drink. And then it seems as if they have all the time in the world to relax.

But today for most weekend-marriage couples, evenings are less a sitcom and more an episode of *Survivor*. It's not just that you're tired. You're also overloaded from the stresses of the day. But then what you're facing isn't hours of relaxation. It's chores. And duties. And responsibilities. Kids. The phone. Aaaarrrrggggghhhh!

What it often feels like is you come home, you walk in the door, and you're swept up by rapids. Eventually you get through it. But irritation and exhaustion make it hard to create any positive energy in your relationship.

Successful weekend-marriage couples don't live the fantasy life that Ricky and Lucy do. They face the same rapids as the rest of us. But instead of getting swept away, they build a bridge over the rapids.

INSIGHT FOR ACTION

Your evening should be a bridge from where you both start out—tired and irritable—to where you want to end up: relaxed, refreshed, and having some moments of closeness with each other. This means dealing with your need to be replenished so you can have some kind of fun or intimacy later. Your priority should be to do whatever it takes to bring positive energy to your relationship.

How do successful weekend-marriage couples do it?

Like all good bridge builders, they think about where they're coming from and where they want to end up.

At the end of the day most of us walk in the door totally frazzled. What works best is to take some time for yourself. I'll talk about what to do if you have small kids in a moment. But if you don't have kids or your kids are older, then doing whatever you need to do to take care of yourself comes first.

This can require a **guerrilla tactic:** When you first come home, ignore each other. Oh, sure, you say, "Hi, how was your day?" But no long sad stories. Then leave each other alone for a while.

This is a miniversion of recharging your batteries. It's better to recharge for two hours so you really have something to give for a half hour than to pick at each other in a state of low emotional energy. You're leaving each other alone not to disconnect from each other, but to build a bridge to later in the evening, when you'll be able to connect with each other.

What makes this confusing is the fact that different people can have different needs when they come home in the evening. Some people's biggest need is to be left alone and recharge their batteries. What other people need when they're under stress is to jump in there and micromanage all the little details so they know that everything's taken care of. That's the only way they can give themselves the peace of mind they need to relax. Still others need quiet companionship—they need quiet after all their stress, but they need companionship because they've been lonely. Lots of people feel lonely after a long, hard day at work. Maybe they've been surrounded by people but the contact has all been businesslike and impersonal. And other people are hungry for more intense contact. These are people who, for example, want to make love right away when they come home or meet their spouse after work for a romantic dinner.

Weekend-marriage couples get into trouble when they don't want the same things when they get home. They might be perfectly suited for each other in every other way *(Isn't it wonderful how we both love old movies?)* but the stress and fatigue of the evening reveals this one area of poor fit *(I know you want to talk to someone when you come home, but can't you see that I'm all talked out?).*

Unfortunately, weekday evenings are the only time you have to be together during the week, and so this small area of poor fit gets enormously magnified. Fortunately, though, I have a lot of experience with this issue. Here's what's most likely to build a bridge from stress and fatigue to fun and intimacy.

Suppose you're in a relationship where by the time you both get home one needs time for herself and the other is eager to connect right then and there. Whose needs get met first? Let me play King Solomon. It's just a big old mistake for two people to try to connect when one is needing to recharge his or her batteries. The one who's needing to recharge is either going to push herself to connect and then resent it or she's going to seem as though she has nothing to give and her spouse is going to resent having to pull teeth to get anything from her.

Where will the positive energy come from if one person's batteries are low? If you're the person who's generally eager for connection, you'll need to understand that the connection will be way better if you wait until your spouse has more to give.

What about those people who have a need to jump in and micromanage all the loose ends when they come home stressed and tired? Why are they bossing everyone around when they really need to lie down? It's for the same reason some people can't relax after dinner until the dishes are washed. We all have to get what we need to relax, and this is what these people need. I know because I'm one of them.

So what do you do if someone who needs to micromanage first and someone who needs to chill first come home from work at the same time? What usually happens is that the micromanager lands on the need-to-chill guy like a ton of bricks and a huge fight ensues.

It's King Solomon time again. In my experience it never works to tell the micromanager to wait until her spouse has recharged his batteries. She'll just get frantic and bug her spouse until a fight starts that uses up the rest of that evening and spoils the next few evenings. Instead, the micromanager needs to be given the ring-master's whip first thing for the sake of her sanity, but for the sake of all that's holy and decent there's got to be a time limit on it. Something like a half an hour is the outside limit. You can manage a lot of micros in a half an hour. What the person who needs to chill gets is the sense of safety that comes with knowing that the micromanaging is time limited.

Here, then, is the sequence that works best. Recharge your batteries first. Then take care of chores and business (unless one of you needs to micromanage to let go of stress and then chores and business come first). Then quiet companionship to settle into being comfortable with each other. Then you'll be ready for more intense contact, whether that means doing something that's fun together or making love or being intimate in some other way.

Where does dinner fit into all this?

Remember how I said at the very beginning that creating positive energy for the relationship is the number-one priority for successful weekend-marriage couples? You can see that in how they deal with dinner compared to the rest of us. The mistake most of us make is to place dinner as the centerpiece of the evening. It's all about the dinner. It doesn't matter how much time it takes or how much stress it causes.

Now this probably made sense in the world of *Meet Me in St. Louis.* Father got home at six. He relaxed with a cocktail and the newspaper until dinner at seven or eight, which was relatively stress free because there was someone to cook it and serve it for the family (although it was probably far from stress free for the cook!). But who lives like that nowadays? We're all household help in our own homes today.

As a result, for many of us, dinner drains positive energy rather than adding to it. Don't misunderstand me. There are plenty of exceptions to this. There are people who manage to throw together a family dinner without breaking a sweat. They may love to cook together, and then they all sit down and have a great time. But while this is the image of what we expect, it's the exception in reality.

Here's the **guerrilla tactic.** Successful weekend-marriage couples make dinner the servant of love. That means that they look at what's easiest, least stressful, most conducive to relaxing and eventually getting close. The result is some very creative solutions. Let me give you some examples.

Some couples feed the kids first and then when the kids are in bed they have dinner together.

Some couples refuse to cook during the week. Dinners are all takeout, order-in, or grab what you can from the fridge.

Some couples use an even more radical **guerrilla tactic.** They just fend for themselves. They say, *How does it help us relax and get close to bang into each other in the kitchen, sit there trying to talk with our mouths full, and then have to be busy cleaning up? Let's let each of us get fed on his own.* Obviously this tactic isn't for everyone. But it can free up a lot of time. Ask yourself this: if you have only a half an hour to be with the person you love, would you rather spend it in bed or at opposite ends of the dinner table?

The key point is that you can't let habit or image trump your need to create positive energy every evening. Let me put it like this. One day when you're one of those cute old couples dodder-ing along the beach in Miami, do you think you'll look back and say, "We sure had some pleasant evenings but, you know, I wish we'd had more real dinners?" Or will you say, "We sure had some nice dinners but I really wish we'd had more pleasant evenings?" Which is it going to be? A lifetime of nice dinners? Or a lifetime of pleasant evenings? Food? Or love? It's your choice, but you need to appreciate that you have a choice.

And why can't you have both? Wait a minute—I thought you told me you were living the weekend marriage. There is rarely time for both.

How do kids fit into managing your frantic evenings? I think most working parents today would say that they can easily spend three hours a night devoted to their kids, cooking for them, bathing them, supervising homework, playing with them, reading to them, talking to them. Of course it varies by age, but my expe-rience tells me that each additional kid adds about a half an hour to this.

Let me offer you some tips that make a big difference accord-ing to successful weekend-marriage couples.

Put the kids to bed as early as possible. Because getting the kids to bed can be such a chore, some parents delay, letting the kids stay up later than they should. This takes away from couple time in the evening and it makes the mornings more stressful because the kids are tired and don't want to get up. From the time your kids are very little, train them in an early-to-bed-early-to-rise habit.

Avoid spending time where both parents are with one kid. You can call it "family time," but for weekend-marriage couples it's a waste. What works best is while one parent is with one kid, the other parent takes care of another child or does chores. Caution: it builds a lot of resentment if one parent does all the child care and the other parent does nothing.

As much as possible, have a fixed routine. Kids are born conservatives. They love having everything be the same way all the time. This works in your favor. The more predictable the routine, the more easily your child will flow with it. The less resistance from your child, the more time and positive energy you have for each other.

Never let your kids become an excuse for your not being together. Kids are time sponges: they will soak up as much of your time as they can. Nothing's easier than for weekend-marriage couples to be so drained from kid time that there's nothing left for couple time. What you have to do, as much as you love your kids, is budget in an absolute minimum of couple time and then do your parenting chores around that.

Guerrilla tactics. As with all guerrilla tactics, this might not be for everyone. But if your evenings are truly gruesomely busy, you might want to try what has worked beautifully for some weekend-marriage couples. What you do is get up an hour or so earlier in the morning. You bring the coffee back to bed and have an hour to hang out when you're in a relaxed frame of mind. So what if you have to go to bed an hour earlier? You're just borrowing an hour from the tired, stressed-out part of your day and giving it to the part of your day when you're rested and refreshed and everything's quieter.

This tactic takes some getting used to. Most couples report that it can take several tries before they adjust. But then it works great.

HEALING THE HURTS

Chapter Thirteen

STRESS-PROOFING YOUR WEEKEND MARRIAGE

Most weekend-marriage couples say that their relationship suffers from too much anger. It could be the kind that shows itself in loud fights, with lots of yelling, name calling, slammed doors. It could be the kind that shows itself in long-simmering fights, with endless bickering and sniping. Or it could show itself mostly in sometimes-prickly, sometimes-polite, but always-frozen distance.

No one in a relationship likes fighting, anger, and distance. But if you're living the weekend marriage, the problem is what to do about it. Many of us wake up each day resolving that from now on there will be harmony. The next thing we know, all the negativity in our relationship is back. The only solution we know, besides swallowing our anger and trying to be nice, is "talking through" our problems. Too often talking things through doesn't help much. What's more, it takes much more time than most weekend-marriage couples have.

Successful weekend-marriage couples have found ways out of this dilemma. They've understood that there have to be ways to prevent anger from building, to deal responsibly with anger once it starts, and to do so in ways that don't use up the precious time they need to spend getting close and enjoying each other. The chapters in this part present these couples' secrets.

WE DID IT *again*. Jack looked at Melissa and she knew he was right—they'd gotten all stressed out and had no one to blame but themselves. It started when they agreed to go to a friend's house for dinner on Thursday night. They'd known that could be a problem because Thursdays were long workdays. And then they had an appointment that had already been rescheduled twice for the bathroom-remodeling guy to be at their house at six-thirty to talk about what they wanted to have done.

They ended up being in a mad rush to get home in time for their appointment with the remodeling guy. Naturally it took longer to talk to him than they'd thought. Then there was a rush to get to their friend's house.

Now here's the deal. I don't know that Jack and Melissa would've had any positive energy for each other that Thursday night after a long workday near the end of a long week. But under the stress of rushing and the fear of being late, then worrying about how much money they were spending on the bathroom, the minute the remodeling guy left, they got into a fight about how Jack hadn't been firm enough in holding down costs. This led to a fight about how Melissa was a critical bitch.

They timed it perfectly: they managed to get out the phrase *I don't even know why we're together anymore* just as they were driving up to their friends' house, certain they'd been keeping everyone waiting.

There's too much stress in all of our lives. I know you know that. But here's something you may not know. A lot of this stress is unnecessary. Come on, don't play victim with me. The stress wasn't all given to you. Like Jack and Melissa, you chose some of it. And if you want your relationship to thrive while you're living the weekend marriage, you're going to have to stop choosing things that bring stress into your life.

And that's because stress is the biggest anger producer around.

I know: we all think we're doing everything we can to reduce stress. But too often we're just kidding ourselves. What really happens is that we have a lot of priorities besides reducing stress, and most of these priorities result in our doing things that actually increase our stress.

And I'm here to tell you that most of those priorities are screwed up. I understand that you're strong and can juggle lots of things. But if you're living the weekend marriage, adding stress to your lack of time puts your relationship at risk. Stress kills. It will not only result in your wearing the marble hat sooner rather than later, but it will also kill your relationship.

INSIGHT FOR ACTION

Most of the stress on weekend-marriage couples comes from saying *yes* when you should've said *no*. So say *no* more often. Whenever anyone asks you to do something, whenever any commitment enters your radar screen, say *no* first unless there's an extraordinary reason for saying *yes*. And whenever you have a choice between a more complicated and a less complicated way of doing things, always choose the less complicated way, no matter what else is involved. Your relationship needs you to do this.

Thinking that we're victims of our stress just adds to our stress. On the other hand, just knowing that you're in the driver's seat reduces stress. When you can step on the gas and put on the brake, you feel more in control.

I know from my own life that sometimes we pay a price when we do things to reduce stress. Sometimes you're going to have to struggle to say *no* when you'd really like to say *yes*. Some people might be a little pissed off for a while. But it's a small price to pay.

Let me help you discover ways to get control of the stress in your life for the sake of your relationship.

Relatives. You may love your parents and get along great with your siblings. If you have kids, relatives can help with the babysitting. But many people find that their relatives are as much a source of stress as of support. Relatives can be critical of you. They can be needy. They can interfere. They can waste your time. And one of the biggest ways that relatives waste your time is by sucking you and your spouse into agonizing discussions about what to do about them.

Take Michelle's mother-in-law, Dorothy. She insisted that Michelle and Bob start coming for dinner on Friday nights. But Michelle knew that they'd be completely exhausted at the end of their tough workweeks. And Dorothy inevitably would have some chore she needed help with. And then Michelle and Bob's evening would be shot. Besides, they usually saw Dorothy on Monday nights. It's enough already!

But Michelle felt guilty. Dorothy's a lonely widow. Michelle wishes she had more time for her. Interestingly, Bob doesn't feel guilty saying *no* even though she's his mother. He has had it up to here with Dorothy. He loves her but she has interfered too much. And he has had to listen to Dorothy criticize Michelle when Michelle wasn't there to stand up for herself.

So Bob and Michelle had a big fight about whether to go. Then they ended up going anyway.

Let's add up the points Michelle and Bob get for stress. Guilt gets a couple of points. The fight gets several points. The fact that they faced a deadline about whether to go or not gets a lot of stress points. And being there—forget about it!

We can't afford this much stress when we're living the weekend marriage. Stress acts on us like a toxic substance. Even a small dose of it lingers. It's not all gone when we wake up the next morning. It takes a while to get over, but time is exactly what you don't have.

Stress is toxic because of what it really is. Stress is essentially fear that you can't take care of yourself. It's anger at everyone who has made it hard for you to take care of yourself. It's depression at the thought that you're going to keep on not being able to take care of yourself. And when someone's afraid, angry, and depressed, he withdraws inside his armor and shoots cannon fire at his spouse. When a couple is experiencing stress, both of them are doing this. Two people turn into two battleships. All because, like Michelle, you couldn't say *no* instead of *yes* to Friday-night dinner at your mother-in-law's.

Guerrilla tactics. Couples have trouble saying *no* because they make it very personal. How can you say *no* to your dear, sweet mother-in-law when all she wants to do is cook you a nice dinner? That's stressful, saying *no* to her face like that! But what successful weekend-marriage couples do is make saying *no* a matter of policy. For example, you could decide that you'll go over to her house for dinner once a month, or whatever time is right for you. Announce it to her directly: "Dorothy, things are really crazy with me and Bob these days what with work and the kids and everything, and we're exhausted. So we've decided that we have to limit ourselves to coming over for dinner once a month." Maybe she'll argue or complain a little. But the big thing is that you've freed up some time and lowered your stress level. And that's always a good thing.

When it comes to relatives, setting limits as a matter of policy is what it's all about. For example, if there's some obnoxious relative, you screen his calls or have a rule that you won't talk to him for more than five minutes.

Have you ever found yourself groaning after a Thanksgiving dinner because you'd eaten too much? But you were the one who kept shoveling in the food. The turkey leg didn't leap off the table and jump down your throat by itself. You were in control. And in the same way, you're in control of saying *no* to stress-producing relatives.

Chores. No question about it: a certain amount of stuff needs to get done in every household. Laundry, dishes, floors. Food has to be shopped for and cooked. Messes need to be straightened out. Bills paid. Now here's what most of us do. We make it our priority to get all the chores done perfectly. Then if there's any time left . . . But too often there isn't any time left. And that means stress. It's stressful to do chores when you need to relax or when you're wanting to spend some time with your spouse. You feel rushed and resentful.

Guerrilla tactics. When it comes to chores, weekend-marriage couples too often get it backward. It's freeing up time that's the important thing. Successful weekend-marriage couples decide on how much time they need to relax and have some space for themselves. Then they do chores in whatever time is left from that. They understand that your life has to work for you. You can't be working for your life.

Here's what will happen if you try this approach. Some chores won't get done, or they won't get done as well as you like. But maybe it won't bother you as much as you feared. Some rooms won't get vacuumed as often. Some meals will be thrown together with more haste than love. Some beds won't get made.

On the other hand, you'll be more relaxed. You'll read a book. You'll get all the way through some magazines that have piled up. You'll go for a few nice long walks. You'll recharge your batteries and have something to give your spouse. Maybe you'll also make love a couple of more times than you would have otherwise. Maybe you'll just hang out together in the living room at night and talk and listen to music.

You see what a sweet deal it can be putting you and your relationship before your chores.

Work. People always say to me, "You don't understand. I don't have any choice about my stress at work."

Maybe you're right. This really is true for some people. Doctors doing their residency. Someone who's trying to get a new restaurant off the ground. People just starting out on a new job. Long-haul truck drivers. Lots of people.

But maybe you're wrong. Most job stress comes from excessive hours, and a lot of people who work extralong hours are doing so unnecessarily. And that's a fact. Some people who work long hours are doing so because they're not organizing their time during the day. Some have volunteered for more tasks than are necessary. Some are needlessly perfectionist. No one will fire them if they come home an hour or so earlier every day starting today.

And lots of times there are changes that can be made over time. Maybe you're working long hours because you have a long commute. A year from now you could be living in a place that saves you two hours a day commuting. That's ten hours a week. Five hundred hours a year. That's like a free gift of twelve work-*weeks* full of time a year. Or maybe you can change jobs. Maybe you can get some help on the job or hand over some of your assignments to someone else. There's almost always a way.

I've seen too many cases where one person working too many hours for too long killed a marriage. That's the weekend marriage with a vengeance. It can easily feel as though days and weeks go by without your seeing each other. The only people who survive a marriage like this are people who prefer a lot of emotional distance in their relationship. But most of us aren't like that.

Friends. What to do about your friends when you're starved for time is a confusing topic. For most of us, friends are a kind of wealth. The more good friends we have, the better. They offer us a way to have fun. They offer support.

But if we're honest with ourselves, we'd acknowledge that friends can sometimes add a lot of stress. We pay a price for this when we're married. I know a lot of couples whose evenings consist of fielding calls from friends. Friends have problems. Friends want to shoot the breeze, and you can't wait to get off the phone. Friends want to make plans, and you have the stress of trying to coordinate things.

And in the end, friends steal time from your relationship. Going out with another couple doesn't count toward intimacy time. It may be a ton of fun. But couples generally don't report that they got closer to each other or felt more intimate after spending an evening with another couple.

Guerrilla tactics. Successful weekend-marriage couples ruthlessly put their relationship first. Tough nuggies to everyone else. This means dropping some friends who aren't much fun. And it means rationing the time they spend with other friends. In other words, it means sometimes saying *no* for the sake of preserving your precious positive energy.

Ambition and perfectionism. If you're going to make a pact with destiny, fine, but know the price you're paying. Lots of people when they're starting out in life make a decision that they're going to rise to the top no matter what it takes, no matter how hard it is. Now here's what a pact like this costs. It will cost you your marriage. Period. The only exception is if you're one of those couples who get along best when you rarely see each other. Some couples are like this, but most aren't.

Now you might point to so-and-so who has risen to the top of some profession or corporation and has a great marriage. I'll make a bet with you. I'll bet this is one of those people whose pact with destiny contains the following clause: *I'll put my heart and soul into my work but only up to a point. There's a certain minimum I'm going to give my relationship and I'm not going to let my professional ambition take anything away from that.* You'd be surprised at how many superachievers made it a top priority to give a certain minimum to their relationship and didn't let even their ambition get in the way of this.

It's up to you. But it's an iron law: if you starve a living thing, it will die. And that includes relationships.

If your ambition is what's primarily responsible for your relationship being so starved for time that it can't survive, then you have a stark choice. If you don't love your spouse, choose ambition. But if you're married to a good person whom you love, choose the marriage. You'll be glad you did.

But what if you're married to someone who's married to his or her ambition? You know how unhappy you are and how your unhappiness is just going to grow and grow. The problem in a situation like this is getting the other person's attention. You can easily seem like a whiny nag, and all that will do is justify in your partner's mind his devoting himself to his ambition. The best solution is to be a teacher, not a nagger. Describe the inevitable deterioration if things keep on the way they're going. Ask him if that's what he wants. Offer to show him ways to dial back his enslavement to his ambition. Talk about specific changes you'd like to make in the ways the two of you relate.

The best thing someone ever said to her obsessively ambitious partner was, "People in our situation who want their marriage to survive end up having a big wake-up call. We can have that wake-up call before a lot of damage has been done or after a lot of damage has been done. Which do you choose?"

Chapter Fourteen

LESS TIME FOR ANGER, MORE TIME FOR LOVE

n a normal relationship, there's nothing wrong with getting mad. Feelings are feelings. A little healthy anger is good for the relationship. It's a way we have of telling the truth and standing up for ourselves and letting our spouse know what's what. And after you get mad, you talk about it, you work things out, you have make-up sex, and then everything's okay.

But you and I don't live in a normal relationship. We live in the weekend marriage. So here's my question: if you don't have much time for your spouse, how much time do you have for anger?

Now I hate it when my husband says, "Don't be angry." I don't want him to tell me how to feel. I don't want him to think that he can do what he wants and then, if I get mad, shut me up by saying, "Don't be angry." So it's hard for me to face the fact that anger's the biggest time-waster around. But it is. For one thing there's all the time you spend expressing your anger. You know how it works. Once you hop on the anger train, you spend a lot of time saying things you don't mean, and then you have to deal with your spouse's saying things he doesn't mean because your getting mad has gotten him mad. Whew!

But once you get on the anger train, you have a lot further to go than that.

Here's the typical after-fight pattern. The person on the receiving end of the anger felt wounded and attacked, even though the other person's feeling wounded and attacked started the whole fight, of course. Terrible things get said in a fight. The person on the receiving end can take days, *weeks,* to feel safe from attack again.

So after wasting time getting mad, you have to waste more time going through a period of coldness. A wall builds up between you with each passing day. And as all of us who've been there know, the more time passes, the thicker the wall gets, and the harder it is to break through. And precious time for love has run through your hands like water through a sieve.

Now let's suppose that a busy couple manages on average to have an hour a day for their relationship. That's actually pretty good for a weekend-marriage couple. Then they get into a huge fight. Most fights like this last a minimum of three hours. So you've immediately used up almost half of your weekly relationship time budget. But it takes at least four times as long to get back to your prefight level of warmth and closeness. The more fights you have, the longer it takes. (That's why some couples end up fighting their way into a lifelong relationship of distance and coldness.)

You can see how one fight can deprive you of positive energy for two or three weeks. But the damage doesn't stop there. Two or three weeks of your relationship being in the dumper will easily make you feel terrible about your relationship. And this makes healing that much harder.

And it always ends with apologies and promises you could've made weeks earlier, saving yourself all this time wasted in pain.

"Is it worth it?" I ask you.

"Is there an alternative?" you ask me.

Of course there's an alternative.

I'm not telling you not to have your feelings. I know how well that works for me! But it's important to prevent yourself from taking that long, stupid, time-wasting journey on the anger train. If you're not careful, you can wake up one day and realize that you've thrown away most of the precious time you've had to love each other.

INSIGHT FOR ACTION

Anger takes up so much time for a weekend-marriage couple that anything you do to reduce the anger that sloshes back and forth between you is worth it. We justify our anger on the grounds that these feelings empower us. But the cost of anger is so high and there are so many alternatives that it's imperative that you try these alternatives. Especially if these alternatives empower you even more.

Now there are two ways to reduce anger in your relationship. The first is fast and powerful, but it's definitely not for everyone. If you can make it work for you, that's the way to go. If not, do the second. It takes a little more work but it's more in line with what's possible for most people.

The first way to deal with anger is a serious **guerrilla tactic:** *don't express anger in your relationship.* I know some of you are saying only someone like Jesus or Gandhi could do this. I know it's very hard for me to do it. But I'd be doing you a disservice if I didn't mention that there are plenty of people who've said, "You know, we're wasting so much precious time and destroying so much positive energy with all the anger in our relationship. So let's go cold turkey. Let's just keep our anger to ourselves when we can. If we have to, let's avoid interacting when we're mad. If there's an important issue to discuss and we're afraid it's going to get contaminated with anger, let's write notes or e-mail and leave out the anger."

Here are ways to help make this guerrilla tactic work.

Eliminate as many sources of anger in your life as possible. That particularly means eliminating stress.

Be vigilant about protecting your spouse from anger you have about things unconnected to him. It's bad enough getting mad because he came home late and didn't call. It's that much worse to get mad at him because you're mad at your boss.

Take some of the energy you'd use getting mad at your spouse to think of ways to accept your spouse. For example, he left the toilet seat up in the middle of the night yet again. You've talked to him about this a million times. But think about it. He either hates you and is involved in a sinister plot to destroy you. Or this is the limit of his ability to change. You've tried to change him. It hasn't worked. Why not admit defeat? You can't win them all. And then why be mad about something you can't change?

Don't think you have to be perfect at no longer expressing anger. No one's perfect at this. But this guerrilla tactic works even if you eliminate only a part of the anger you used to express.

Don't confuse not expressing anger with not dealing with problems. Deal with your problems, but keep anger out of it.

Here's the second way to reduce anger in your relationship: *prevent unnecessary anger.* This is the ecological approach. You understand that anger is perfectly natural, but so are weeds, and if you can prevent weeds from growing in your garden, you can do things to prevent anger from growing in your relationship. You'll be surprised how do-able this is. It turns out that there are lots of things you can do.

You can prevent the anger from happening in the first place. To see how to do that, let's look at the anatomy of fights.

We get angry because we're shocked and frustrated. That's why we so often launch our flight of anger by saying, "I can't believe you . . ." This element of *disbelief* and *disempowerment* in anger is the essential clue to what's really going on in a fight.

Here's one scenario:

Michael and Viv led a pretty active social life, always going out to parties and dinner engagements. They also went to the theater a lot. Many of the functions they went to were connected to Michael's business. It was often important for them to be where they were going on time. Michael would always say something like "Honey, they're expecting us at eight. With traffic and everything we'd better not leave a minute later than seven-fifteen."

"Okay, honey," Viv would always say.

Then, sure as shooting, Michael would be standing in the living room at 7:15 shouting upstairs, "Honey, we've got to leave right now."

And Viv would shout back, "I'll be right down." Maybe she would be down in a minute. Maybe it would take her another half hour.

The fight would start on the walk to the car and Michael would use a line that occurs in about half of all fights: "My God,

I've asked you a million times . . ." In this case he'd asked Viv a million times to be ready at the agreed-upon hour. Half of all fights arise because one spouse has asked the other a million times to do or stop doing something, but he or she still hasn't complied. The anger comes from the sense of disbelief and disempowerment. It feels outrageous and humiliating that after asking so many times, after asking *nicely* so many times, your need would still be ignored. *How is this possible?*

Then at some point, of course, you snap. This is an inevitable component of these *I've asked you a million times* fights. You're patient, you hang in there, and then you just can't take it anymore. You erupt.

Here's the other scenario:

It was Sally's twenty-ninth birthday. This was a big deal for her. The next one would be the big three-oh, a painful milestone for a lot of people. Sally looked at turning twenty-nine as her last birthday as a young woman.

And Ben forgot it. Sure, he was caught up in a project at work. Sure, Sally's last couple of birthdays kind of blurred together as not very meaningful. Sure, Sally hadn't given particularly clear hints. *But who forgets their spouse's birthday—flat out forgets it?* It's unthinkable. Unheard of.

Ben hadn't said anything in the morning. Sally had thought, *Well, maybe he's just trying to fake me out.* But that night Ben came home later than usual and said, "Hey Sal, I'm home. Sorry I'm late. It was crazy at work today. Do we have any dinner ready?"

This was no fake-out. He'd blown her off completely. And this is when Sally used the line people use in the other half of all fights: "How could you have . . ." She said, "How could you have forgotten my birthday? I've had four birthdays since we've been together. This is not a big surprise for you. You just forgot? No one forgets something like this." And Sally got angrier and angrier as she saw poor stupid Ben standing there half-dazed with guilt, half-trying to convince Sally that she was making too big a deal out of this.

This is the other half of all fights. These occur when someone outrageously steps over an obvious boundary. There's usually a feeling of deep humiliation. You've done something that everyone knows you just can't do. And that means that you feel that you've treated your spouse like a nothing. Again there's that feeling of disbelief and disempowerment. And of course fear. If your spouse could forget your birthday, call you a terrible name, kiss your best friend on the lips at the Christmas party, lose all that money in the stock market, buy that car without talking to you— then he or she needs a wake-up call because who knows what could happen next.

That's how fights are conceived in the womb of disbelief and disempowerment. And the impetus is almost always either crossing some line you've been warned about a million times or else committing some outrageous act.

So if you want to prevent anger from coming up in the first place, then beware of committing outrages and beware of situations where your spouse has talked to you about something a million times and you still don't change.

There's nothing brilliant to say about committing outrages beyond *don't do it*. But you can protect yourself by constantly checking in with what is most important to your spouse. When people get really busy, they often lose sight of that. They also lose a sense of connection to each other. That leads people to commit outrages that come from their wanting to see what they can get away with. So staying connected to each other is an important part of preventing outrages.

Here's what to do about situations where one of you has been asked to do something a million times and still hasn't changed. *You need to talk about what the hell is going on here.*

Maybe you have inappropriate expectations. The most obvious reason why someone doesn't do something you've asked them to do a million times is that it's quite literally impossible for them. It may not be impossible for other people, but you and I have real blind spots sometimes. Marriage has a way of uncovering these things that are just impossible for some of us. And if that's the case, all you can do is let it go and find a way to work around it.

Maybe your spouse doesn't know how important this is to you. This always comes as a shock to people. Wouldn't your spouse know how important it was to you if you've told him a million times? But the mistake lots of people make is to use anger as a way of conveying importance. Your spouse has a much better chance of understanding *how* important this is to you if you calmly explain *why* it's important.

Maybe your spouse doesn't know what to do to change. People who are habitually late, for example, try to be ready on time and for some reason it always eludes them in spite of their best efforts. They need a patient tutor. They need someone who can help them debug the places they get hung up.

Maybe you haven't talked to your spouse about how you can help him change. If you said something a million times, this is obviously something that's hard for your spouse. If it's important enough for you to get mad about, it's important enough for you to hang in there and be helpful.

That's how to prevent anger from occurring.

Now suppose the anger has already started. Your spouse is upset, which could easily lead to a lot of anger and a big fight. Here are some tools for soothing anger that's already gotten under way. Each one reduces anger by a significant percentage. Let's take them one at a time.

Listen. There's an entire chapter later on how to listen. It's important for you to understand now that listening is one of the best ways to prevent anger. Let's say your spouse is upset about something. You could argue, try to talk her out of it, get mad yourself because she's pushed your buttons. But all this will do is turn being upset into being angry.

Suppose you listened. Then maybe you'd find out why she's upset. What this means to her. What she needs. If necessary, you could ask questions to get at this. Listening takes the anger out of being upset—the issue is still there but the potential damage that comes from anger has been eliminated.

Know that you have a choice, but it will always play out the same way: you can stoke your spouse's anger by not listening or you can soothe her anger *permanently* by doing a really good job of listening. It's up to you!

Use do-overs. This is the magic anger eraser. Let's say you were stupid enough to say, "What the hell were you thinking when you . . . ?" Then your spouse says, "Take a do-over," or "Take two," or "Try that again." It's amazing how effective this is. Instead of spiraling into more anger, the two of you are given a second chance to deal with the same material in an anger-free way.

Liz told me that saying this always worked with her husband: "Let's stop this. I mean it. We're starting a big fight here and I don't think either of us wants to have a fight right now. Let's try this again without having a fight."

Never make a unilateral move. A "unilateral move" is when you do something without consulting your spouse. I'm not talking about buying a stick of gum. I'm talking about your doing something that has a real impact on your spouse and her life. If so, you have to include her upfront. Spending more than an agreed-upon amount of money. Quitting your job. Inviting your mother to come and live with you. You get the point. These are the kinds of things where if you do them on your own (unilaterally), your spouse will go, "You did what!?! And without talking to me first!?!"

Do what you say you're going to do. Few things make people angrier than feeling betrayed. This is because trust is such a fundamental need. Now your spouse understands that you're not perfect. She can factor it in that you sometimes forget to take out the garbage without being reminded, for example. She can trust that you will usually take out the garbage. But if you make a promise—and saying that you're going to do something is a promise—then her continuing to trust you depends on your doing that. Not sometimes. Not maybe. Not partially. Just doing it. *Don't promise anything you can't deliver. And if you make a promise, then you must deliver it.*

Any time you violate an agreement or don't keep your word,

you're not doing what you said you'd do. It's much better to promise less than you think you can deliver, even if it initially disappoints your spouse, than to promise more and disappoint your spouse big time.

Don't be mean. No one means to be mean. But we are. Sometimes it's because our brains are disconnected from our tongues. Sometimes it's because we're trying to drive a point home. Sometimes it's because we want to be left alone. But there's no excuse. There's nothing you can do in a mean way that you can't do more effectively in a respectful or kind way.

It's easy to be led into being mean. If you say, "God, you're such a jerk," you'd think you'd get your spouse's attention and make your point at the same time. You'd think it would be a time-saver. But it works just the opposite way. In reality, you've *diverted* his attention away from your need and on to your meanness. Now the two of you are off and running, playing the anger game.

Don't escalate. Here's what it means to escalate: your spouse throws gasoline on the floor and you say, "Oh yeah?" and then throw a lighted match. In our stressed-out, time-starved lives, we escalate with words all the time. Someone gets a little mad, the other gets a lot madder. A little threat leads to a larger threat. A mild insult leads to a horrible insult. People tell me they do this because of a feeling of not wanting the other person to "get away with" whatever he's doing. But as you know from the political stage, all escalating accomplishes is more escalating.

It's impossible to say what words to use instead of escalating. It so much depends upon the situation. But my husband used to escalate a lot and he's gotten a lot better. Here's what he tells me he does: "I just think about what I'm about to say or do and if I think it's going to add fuel to the fire, I don't say or do it. Then I don't say anything until I can think of something that won't add fuel to the fire, and I say that."

Never mind-read or psychoanalyze. Have you ever told someone what you wanted and they responded by telling you that what's really going on is that you want something else? It made you pretty mad, didn't it? No one likes to be told, *I know you better than you know yourself.* This is really ascribing hidden motives. If your spouse says what she needs or how she feels, prevent anger by taking her at face value. You can, if you want, ask her if that's all she needs. But that's just doing a good job of listening. Don't ever play psychoanalyst.

Say you're sorry. Women tell me men rarely say they're sorry. Men tell me that women say they're sorry too late. Let's just say we all need to say we're sorry more often and sooner.

The reason we don't say we're sorry is that we feel attacked and we feel the attack isn't fair. Saying you're sorry would be like confessing to a crime you didn't commit. But a relationship isn't a court of law. It's a place where two people bring as much positive energy as they can to improve things. *I'm sorry* doesn't function as an admission of guilt. It shows you care, that you see your spouse is hurting, that you feel badly about her distress. *I'm sorry* is not about you at all. It's about what your spouse needs.

Show your spouse that you understand where she's coming from. If anger is a way of turning up the volume, you can get your spouse to turn down the volume by showing you hear her without anger. The best way to do this is to show that you understand why this issue is so important to her. The mistake we make is to deal with an angry person by trying to show them that what's so important to them shouldn't be important. This is when we use classic phrases like "I don't see why you're making such a big deal about this. You're getting angry over nothing."

Instead say, "I really do understand why this is so important to you." Then say something that shows that you really do understand. If you can't think of anything, then just repeat what she's said.

Say, "You're right." Particularly when we're pressed for time, we get mad when we think someone doesn't agree with us. This just broadens your sense of disagreement. It's called polarization. People who study relationships have known for decades how easy it is for two people in a relationship to start a little apart and end up feeling very far apart. Here's why this is stupid. People typically fight as though they're in 100 percent *dis*agreement when in fact they're in 90 percent *a*greement. What a time-waster!

So first find the agreement; then work out the small part where you don't agree. And you can do this by identifying all the ways you think your partner is right.

Be helpful. Most anger is a cry for help. It's a way of saying, *Ouch, I have a problem.* So if you respond to someone who's getting mad by saying, "How can I help?" or "What do you need?" your spouse will see that you're being constructive, not obstructive.

For example, Tina was sick and tired of hearing her husband grouch about how they were spending money like water. Naturally she was fed up with Nick's making it seem that it was all her fault. But blaming Nick didn't help either. Nick's anger was diffused when Tina said, "Look, I know this is a big problem. Let's sit down and talk about what we can do. Tell me what you need to stop worrying so much."

Ask when would be a good time for the two of you to talk about this. We usually feel ambushed by our spouse's anger. It hits us at the wrong time. (Is there ever a right time?) But people *hate* to be told, "I don't want to talk about it." They feel shut up. That just makes them more angry. At the same time, it will make you mad to talk about this when it's not a good time for you. You can solve two problems at once by asking your spouse when he'd like to talk about it with you. Then make sure you do it. There's something very satisfying about having an appointment to deal with an important issue.

Chapter Fifteen

SOLVING PROBLEMS FAST

Normal couples sit down and talk whenever they have to make a decision ("Shall I take that job offer even though it means moving to New York?") or solve a problem ("What are we going to do about Jimmy's learning disability?"). Weekend-marriage couples don't have time to sit down, much less talk. So decisions don't get made. Problems don't get solved. And when they do talk, it's so rushed and stressed that they think twice before talking again.

Take Seth and Sarah. Even good things can become problems for weekend-marriage couples because we don't have the time to talk about what to do and how to do it. Seth and Sarah were looking forward to their fifth anniversary. It was a big deal for them. With both sets of parents divorced, it felt like an important milestone to make it this far.

It was especially important for Sarah. She felt she'd been cheated out of the wedding she'd dreamt of. She and Seth had been living together for a few years. Suddenly there was an opportunity to buy a house they could afford, and even more suddenly they decided they wanted to get married before moving in. But there wasn't the time or money to do it right. And Sarah gave up the big wedding she'd always wanted.

So now Sarah started putting pressure on Seth to do something really, really, *really* great for their fifth anniversary. Like go on a trip-of-a-lifetime to Paris. But Seth was in his last year of medical residency. He was incredibly busy and money was tight. He wanted Sarah to be happy, but none of the plans Sarah was talking about made him happy.

And their relationship was in one of those queasy places weekend marriages get to. Sarah and Seth were both busy, tired, stressed-out people. Seth just wanted to collapse in the evening like an old dog after a long run. About a year earlier, Sarah had opened a funky little woman's clothing boutique. It was doing well. But when Sarah came home in the evening she was in a strange state. She was starved for connection. But she was also very irritable.

Sarah and Seth found that if they talked about things, they'd soon get into a fight. Sarah claimed that Seth didn't really ever want to talk about anything. Seth claimed that he was perfectly content to talk about stuff but why did it always have to be so difficult and complicated and intense?

So they had these talks that were more like fights and that accomplished little. Meanwhile their fifth anniversary was rushing at them like a giant truck.

Most weekend-marriage couples feel like Sarah and Seth. How do you figure out what to do when you have different needs and little time to figure out a way to bridge those differences? It's easy when you need the same thing at the same time. And we get spoiled because we often fall in love with someone precisely because it seems we do have the same needs at the same time. But I'm sure even thirty thousand years ago a caveman and cavewoman fought because he wanted to go out hunting bears and she said, "You're always out hunting bears. Why don't you stay home and help me gather nuts and berries."

Now, by some kind of cruel joke, when we have so many resources and so many options, we don't have time to talk our way to a good and fair solution. At least it seems that way. After all, most of us have the experience in our relationships that it too often takes hours and hours of talking to work out any kind of agreement at all.

You know how weekend-marriage couples live? It's a needless mess. Either decisions never get made at all and you just drift along not dealing with what needs to be dealt with, or there's some kind of fight and an abrupt and unsatisfying solution is grabbed hold of, usually marked by the words "Fine, if that's what you want." Or someone just goes ahead and does whatever he wants and leaves the other person to deal with it.

This is a mess because you're just not getting fast, good, and fair agreements that two halfway intelligent people should be able to come up with. And when needs aren't met and decisions aren't made, the relationship turns into this miserable drifting raft of squabbling castaways.

But it's a needless mess, because any two people, no matter how busy they are, can arrive at the solutions they need. You just have to know the shortcuts that work when you're living the weekend marriage.

HERE'S WHAT *DOESN'T* work. You guys can no longer afford to indulge in relaxed, unstructured conversations about issues that you hope will somehow miraculously bring you to clarity. Maybe you could do that when you were first together and had a lot more time. But not now. Now you sit down to "just talk" and a half an hour later you're no closer to clarity than when you started. Actually a half an hour is usually just long enough to bring out how far apart you seem to be. *But you've run out of time.*

It's nuts! It would be like starting a meal that takes an hour of preparation time when you have only a half hour for preparing and eating combined. You'd have nothing but two starving people surrounded by piles of half-prepared dishes. Which is exactly what we have when it comes to the solutions we're hungry for.

HERE'S WHAT DOES work. You'll recognize it as a three-step procedure you already use with friends, on the job, everywhere:

1. You each say what you need.

Now you do *not* spend any time arguing with each other about why what the other person needs is stupid. I realize that it would be an enormous time-saver if you could say, "Your needs are stupid," and your spouse would smack himself on the forehead and say, "My gosh you're right, thanks for pointing that out to me." Discussion avoided! But in fact this is not a time-saver because no one ever thinks their needs are stupid. It's a time-waster because you're arguing over something that can't change.

And you do *not yet* talk about solutions. If you try to talk about solutions at this early stage, you'll just waste time because you don't know enough yet to be smart.

And if you don't know what you need, be careful. This is not the time to think about solving problems and making decisions. You need to do something different. You need to explore what your needs are. Here's the best way to do that. Think. Talk to friends. Go over the situation in your mind and ask yourself what you need. Sit with this process of discovery until your needs become clear. Then you can have a conversation with your partner about what to do.

2. Next, after you've both said what you need, spend some time bringing out the most important issues about this decision or problem—your feelings, important facts, your priorities. You can call this *kicking around the ball*. You're exploring. Opening things up. What's great is that you can do this really fast if you're not talking each other out of your needs or prematurely squabbling over solutions.

3. *Now* one of you pulls together some solution that does a pretty good job of balancing all this. The other can add or change some things to make the solution work better.

Make sure you follow through with whatever you've agreed on.

What's great about this little procedure is that you can use it to *quickly* arrive at good decisions. The less time you have, the better it can work for you. Remember: the essence of it is that you both say what you need, then you explore the situation, and then a decision emerges from that exploration.

Let's see how Seth and Sarah could use it.

First Sarah would let Seth know what she really needs about this fifth anniversary that's so important to her. The mistake Sarah made was painting these elaborate pictures of the kind of celebration that would make her happy. She wanted Seth to understand her dream. She wanted to make sure he didn't think he could get away with some el-cheapo solution.

But what ended up happening was that Seth got scared. Worse than that, Sarah did herself a disservice. She *wanted* something like a trip to Paris. But what she really *needed* was something special and memorable. And that's all Sarah had to say at the beginning: "I can give you some examples, but as long as what we do is special and memorable, that's all I need."

Lots of times once you've said what you need, you're done. Mission accomplished. Now your spouse knows exactly what you need. And maybe he can agree to it immediately.

File this under strange but true: people complain a lot in their relationships but no one knows what the other needs. How can this be? Because by the time you've heard the complaining, you can't hear the need. You're overloaded, confused, and pissed off. Of course the reason we complain before we say what we need is that by the time we are able to pinpoint what we need, *we* are feeling overloaded, confused, and pissed off. And we want our spouse to know it.

Now what would you do if you learned that your spouse wouldn't be able to hear your need because she was overloaded from listening to your complaining? Maybe you'd complain anyway. Maybe getting this grievance off your chest is the most important thing for you. Maybe nothing will feel more satisfying than being heard.

But probably what you really need most is for your spouse to hear what you need. If so, here's a **guerrilla tactic.** Skip the complaining. Just state your need as simply as possible. Period.

Let's say it's a Saturday and your spouse says he has to run to the store. "I'll be right back," he says. But he's gone for four hours. You spent that whole time waiting for him, unable to make plans.

What do you need? You need him, before he goes out, to give you an accurate statement in advance of how long he's going to be out. If a problem should come up, he should call you.

Now what should you say? "Next time if you're going to be out, before you leave I need you to give me an estimate of how long you'll be gone and to call if it's longer than that." And that's it. The point is that you shouldn't waste your breath or test your spouse's patience with explanations, harangues, and complaints. Just state your specific need about this one issue.

Then do this. Ask, "Do you promise you'll do that?" Don't end the conversation until you get the promise.

Now your spouse might try to wriggle out of making a promise: "Well, I'll try, but I don't always have control over [blah, blah, blah]." Now you've got to make a judgment call here. Is he really just wriggling out? Or is he bringing up a realistic issue? If it's a realistic issue, then either solve it or live with it. If you can sense he's trying to wriggle out, just say, "Look I need you to promise you're going to do your best."

The point is that when you're living the weekend marriage, you have time to focus only on your needs, not on all the negativity surrounding them.

Sometimes, of course, there's more to it than just your saying what you need. You have to try to find a way to fit two people's needs together.

To go back to our example, the next thing to happen is that

Seth would say what he needed. What Seth had been doing was whining and complaining. "It's too expensive. . . . We don't have any time for a trip. . . . You're too extravagant." But Seth never bothered saying what he needed, like, for example, "I need us to have a nice anniversary, too. But we can't take more than a week off and we can't afford to spend more than three thousand dollars."

Now here comes the all-important step. Once you've both said what you need, and before you jump to solutions, you ought to bring out the issues that are most important to each of you. This is one of those things that are confusing for weekend-marriage couples. It seems to take time to air out the issues. But this is one place where you save time by spending time.

Here's how it might go. Seth and Sarah would go for a walk or drive to their favorite coffeeshop. Sarah would talk about how, with Seth being so busy, she was starting to feel deeply disconnected from him. She was hoping for a vacation that would really bring them closer. If Seth listened carefully, he'd get the point: this wasn't about Sarah's being extravagant. It was about Sarah's wanting to do something important for their relationship.

Just as important, by talking about what mattered to them they avoided the huge mistake of trying to talk the other person into not needing what he or she needs. This is always a mistake. When you tell people they shouldn't need what they need, they feel as if you're attacking their very selves with a sledgehammer. That would make anyone pretty defensive!

Fortunately, it's much easier to find a solution that does a pretty good job of meeting both your needs than to change anyone's needs.

This might help. Whenever one of you says what you need,

think of it like a walnut. The walnut shell is Sarah's saying "I need to go to Paris for my anniversary." The shell is useless, but it focuses all your attention. Instead, you have to figure out her real need. That's the meat inside. It might be "I need us to do something memorable for this anniversary."

Now when you want to get the meat out of a walnut shell, you squeeze it until it cracks. Or you just whack it. But you can't do that with your spouse! You can get at his true need by asking questions. Ask your spouse, "Why is this important to you? What is it that makes you care so much about this? What's the one piece of this you would absolutely never want to let go of?" Questions like these bring out the meat of your spouse's need. That's why you need that all-important and ultimately time-saving conversation where you just kick around the problem and your concerns and possible options before you jump to coming up with a solution. You find the need within the need. Then you're in a much better position to find a solution that works.

Sometimes, as you kick things around, it turns out that you both have lots of needs. That's pretty common with weekend-marriage couples. The harder you work and the more pressure you're under, the more unmet needs build up. Then when you start talking about some decision, all those needs fall out onto the table. It can be confusing and discouraging. It's like your weekend marriage in a microcosm. Too many needs at once!

But here's what successful weekend-marriage couples do. They say, *Okay, we have a lot of needs, but they're not all equally important. When I think about it, my top need here is . . .* This is essential. Too many cooks spoil the broth. Too many needs make decision making impossible, particularly when you don't have time.

But in my experience, any solution that satisfies your top one or two needs and your spouse's as well will be almost as good as a perfect solution, and it will take a tenth the time.

Then Seth and Sarah would try to come up with a solution that does a pretty good job of balancing their needs. Usually this happens faster and produces a better solution because you've first spent time kicking things around and listening to each other.

Guerrilla tactics. Let me tell you what a lot of successful weekend-marriage couples do here at the solution stage, and it's great.

Do you like meetings? Do you think they're an incredibly fun, productive way of getting things done? I doubt it! So why would you and your spouse have a meeting to come up with a solution? It's hard to find the time. And then you'll spend it raising niggling objections to each other's ideas and annoying the heck out of each other.

Instead do this. Once you've gotten out your needs and kicked things around, choose one of you to go off and pull together a solution that should make both of you happy. It may not be a perfect or wonderful solution, but it might very well be a darn good one.

What Seth and Sarah would do would be this. When they came home from their walk, Sarah would have the job of drafting a plan for their anniversary vacation that takes full account of Seth's concerns, like his three-thousand–dollar limit on expenses. Sarah's a good person for this because, if they're honest with each other, they recognize that she's the one who cares most about this anniversary. And my motto is: *the one who cares most must dare to prepare.* That way you have the most influence over the final outcome, and that's what you want because you care the most.

But of course Sarah can't lay down the law. She's just coming up with a draft of a proposal. The next step is for Seth to look at the draft and make any changes he feels are necessary. He can add some things to make the solutions work better for both of them. But he can't rewrite the draft. Trust has got to be an important part of this process. If Sarah has the job, Seth should mostly stick to what Sarah comes up with.

I can't tell you how much time and wear and tear it saves to make decisions in this way. It's so fast and easy.

INSIGHT FOR ACTION

A decision is a tool for meeting needs. The mistake weekend-marriage couples make is to spend too little time talking about what they really need and too much time trying to talk each other out of their needs and arguing about the details of specific solutions. The best use of your scarce time is to have a full airing of all your needs. Maybe you go for a walk or sit down for a cup of coffee or for lunch and talk about your needs. Then you kick around whatever issues and concerns are important to you. Then let one of you go off and draft a solution that meets both of your needs. Then you revise it and you're all set.

You have to make sure you follow through with the agreement. This is where weekend-marriage couples often get into trouble. It causes a lot of anger when they see each other not following through. They blame each other for being lazy or not caring about the relationship.

But the best solution isn't to grit your teeth, bear down, and do a better job of following through. The best solution is to come up with a decision that you can both support. So if you find that you're not following through, don't blame each other. Blame the decision. Somehow in the process of coming up with it, you didn't take into account someone's needs or someone else's reality. And now it's come back to bite you in the butt.

REMEMBER WHEN I talked about people who were dogs, people who weren't afraid of confrontation, and people who were ducks, people who hated confrontations? You learned which one you were. This becomes very important for making decisions as a couple because dogs and ducks get into very different kinds of trouble.

Ducks don't make their needs clear. It's too confrontational to say what you need.

Dogs fight too hard for every last one of their needs. They don't appreciate how much these struggles cost.

But look at what happens as a result. Ducks find that over and over again they've agreed to something that they don't like, and that makes them resentful. If Sarah were a duck, she'd say, "You're right, we shouldn't be spending money now. Our anniversary isn't a necessity. We can just have some friends over for dinner." The only problem is that she'd be miserable. And she'd be angry, too, even though Seth had done nothing more than agree to what she said she needed. But Sarah would be angry with Seth anyway because she'd feel that Seth had railroaded her into dinner instead of a trip.

Ducks are always feeling railroaded. If you're a duck, think about how many times you've gotten yourself into trouble by not making what you need clear. I know this is especially hard in the weekend marriage. The pace and pressure of life don't seem to allow us to bring up our needs. But you know a need is important when it generates anger and resentment if it's not met. And you don't have the time to deal with that anger and resentment in the weekend marriage.

The only time-saving measure is to stop being so duckish and let your spouse know exactly what you need.

Dogs find that over and over they push too hard. It feels hard for them not to. After all, when you're still talking about what you're going to do, the possibility of your getting everything you want is dangling there in front of you. It may be a castle in the air, but you genuinely think you have a chance to live in it. All I can say is, "Down, boy." Where has this ever gotten you? If you push too hard, you risk losing everything.

If you're in a relationship with another dog, you know the endless terrible fights the two of you have had trying to decide the slightest thing.

If you're in a relationship with a duck, you know the weird thing that happens. You always get everything you want, and then somehow your spouse eventually gets you for it.

This is why it's so important for the dog to really listen during the part of the discussion where both of you put forward your needs. If the solution you come up with doesn't do a good job of meeting *both* people's needs, then forget about it.

Guerrilla tactics. It seems obvious that if you and your spouse have to make a decision or solve a problem, you'd sit down and talk about it. It's almost an ingrained habit for couples. But talk takes time and leads to tangles.

Here's an incredibly effective alternative many successful

weekend-marriage couples use. You *never* talk about your problems. Instead, you resolve all your problems via written notes or e-mail. Some people hate writing so much that they can't use this tactic. And that's okay. But if you don't mind writing, doing all your problem solving with notes or e-mails means you never spend face-to-face time talking about problems! What a relief.

And this means that you break free of that horrible conditioning weekend-marriage couples get into where you look at your partner's face and immediately think, *Oh my God, we're going to have to talk about problems.* Now you can look at your partner's face and be assured that you'll never be talking about problems.

What's more, by putting everything in writing, everything's clearer, simpler, and less likely to lead to fights. Writing can be a much cooler medium than talking. It's even great for expressing how you feel.

There's one thing you need, though, for this tactic to work well. Just because it's down in black and white doesn't mean that there's anything final about what anyone said. The only problem with writing is that written words can sometimes seem too definite. So you have to understand that the only time you're locked into anything you write is when you call it a final agreement.

Here's how you can use this tactic to make a decision. You send an e-mail about one problem, need, or issue. I have to lay down the law about this: one topic per e-mail. As great as this tactic is, it immediately becomes terrible if you use your e-mails to send laundry lists of demands to each other.

Then the other responds with what he or she needs.

Maybe there are a couple more e-mails back and forth bringing up some of your concerns or offering up information.

Then one of you sends an e-mail with the subject heading "What do you think about this solution?" This is when you propose a solution.

The other responds by fine-tuning that solution.

There have been six e-mails and you've spent far less time than you would have if you'd been talking. Plus you can spread it out in tiny chunks over the week. Plus you can do it at work and have more time for your relationship. It goes without saying that you can do the same thing via handwritten notes.

HERE ARE SOME quick solutions for common problems time-starved couples always ask about making decisions:

"I don't feel it's worth the bother to say what I need. It's too diffi-cult. Nothing's going to come of it. And there's no time, anyway." There are two kinds of needs. Those that pass, such as the need to eat a pizza like the one you just saw on TV. And those that get more intense with time, like the need to eat, period. It's a mistake to always pay attention to the first kind of need. It's a disaster to ignore the second kind of need.

When people get to the point where they feel it's not worth putting forth their needs, they make the mistake of blaming it on their spouse's limitations.

I know what you're going to say: *What mistake? He is limited.*

In my experience, when we think our spouse can't meet our needs, three different things are going on.

First, we haven't gotten their attention. Oh, sure, we've been complaining nonstop. But what complaining does is make other people tune out. Here's how to get your spouse's attention.

Weekend-marriage couples often make the mistake of talking to each other on the fly. Your spouse is doing some chore. Or she's preoccupied with something. And then you toss some important need of yours in the air hoping your spouse is going to grab hold of it. Well, you're deluding yourself. Your spouse is much more likely to casually bat it away like an annoyance. When you're starved for time, the easiest word in the English language to say is *No!*

The magic formula you should use is "Do you have a minute? This is important to me. Here, let's sit down and talk for a bit." Honestly, if you don't feel your need is worthy of getting your spouse to sit down and talk for a few minutes, then you shouldn't be talking to him about it at all. But if it is worthy, then unless you get his attention, you're just setting yourself up for more and more frustration.

Second, you haven't let him know how important your need is to you. I get very sad when I think about all the relationships in which people don't feel loved by their spouses, but their spouses really do love them. They'd do almost anything if they grasped how important a need of theirs was. But it just hasn't been made clear to them.

I think a big reason why your spouse may not know how important your need is is that he doesn't know *why* it's important to you. Seth had trouble grasping how important the fifth-anniversary celebration was for Sarah as long as he thought it was just some girlie thing she was into—you know, not serious to him. But when Sarah explained what it really meant to her given her parents' divorce, he understood.

Here's a great **guerrilla tactic** you can use for conveying quickly how important your need is. Assign a number from 1 to 10. Reserve 10 for your most important needs. For example, "I need you to help more with chores in the evening. And that's a ten for me. We're both tired from a long day but if I'm running around getting dinner and cleaning up and you're playing with the kids, it doesn't feel fair to me. I resent you and then what does that do to our relationship?"

The great thing about assigning a number is that it immediately resolves most discussions. Maybe your spouse had a sweet deal playing with the kids, but when he understands how important it is to you, he might say, "Well, it's only a five for me to play with the kids while you're preparing dinner. I have the whole rest of the evening with them." You're home free.

Third, we haven't shown our spouse exactly how to meet our needs. The problem here is that what seems obvious to us may be a complete mystery to our spouse. We say things like "I need some space," or "I need you to be nice to me," or "I need you to take some responsibility around here." We're sure that we've said something a child could understand.

But despite your having said you need some space, your spouse continues to talk to you. What is he, an idiot? No. He just thought that by "space" you meant that you didn't want him to ask you questions about your day. But it was okay for him to talk as long as he didn't expect you to answer.

When you're living the weekend marriage, the only way to save time and get your needs met is to treat your spouse like a child and spell out everything: "Look, when I say I need space, I mean I really need to be treated like I'm living alone. After all the pressure at work and then coming home to this small apartment,

I get no alone time. I don't need you to leave, but it would feel so great if for a while you would just treat me as if I'm not here. Treat me like I'm invisible. Don't talk to me."

"My spouse is so unreasonable/stingy/extravagant/etc. But I can't seem to get him to change his needs." I have a great solution for this but it's just radical enough to qualify as a **guerrilla tactic**. Never comment on your spouse's needs. Never try to change them. Never get into a discussion about why those needs are crazy, stupid, or whatever. Just accept that they are what they are. This doesn't mean that you go along with everything your spouse needs. If it's unacceptable to you, just say *no.* If it's extravagant, show why you can't afford it.

Deal with your spouse's needs by making clear what it is *you* need. No matter how incompatible your needs seem, there's some solution that both of you can agree to.

But don't try to convince your spouse that there's something wrong with him for needing what he needs. It's hard for most people to say what they need. By the time most people bring a need into their relationship, it's become very important to them. And it's probably important because it has to do with his sense of who he is as a person. His identity is tied up with it. If you attack his need, he'll feel attacked. Then he'll fight back. And you don't have time for the mess this causes.

Doug and Leah had two teenage children. Doug had thought that they'd made a firm agreement that that was that. Imagine Doug's surprise when at age forty-two Leah announced that she wanted to have a baby. To Doug this seemed crazy. He was looking at how much college would cost in the next few years. Almost fifty and a successful lawyer, Doug was dreaming of retirement. A baby was the last thing he wanted.

Doug and Leah had very little time together but soon all of it was taken up with fighting about whether to have a baby. Doug made the classic mistake of trying to convince Leah that she was wrong for needing what she needed. He tried to convince her that she was compensating for something that was missing in her life, that she was doing this as a form of denial about menopause coming one day.

As you can imagine, the more Doug tried to make Leah "see" that her need was crazy, the more she worked at showing how she was justified in needing what she needed. By trying to devalue her needs, Doug was strengthening the very thing he was trying to weaken.

And it wasted so much time.

Once Doug stopped trying to convince Leah not to need what she needed, he focused on saying what he needed, which was not to have a baby in his life.

Before you knew it, after they kicked the issue around a little they found a solution that worked for both of them. With their previous kids Doug had been a very involved parent. Leah promised that this time she wouldn't ask him to do anything that he didn't want to do. She took responsibility for the fact that if she wanted a baby at this time in their lives, she'd have to do most of the work. She kept to her agreement. It was only fair. He'd paid his dues. He didn't want the responsibility of taking care of another kid at his age. And she understood and accepted that. It was worth it for her since she wanted to have another child. They both ended up very happy with their decision.

"Whenever we talk about something, we get into these rambling conversations that go nowhere. We don't have the time for this, and it's discouraging." Every relationship has practical interactions and loving interactions. The less time you have together, the more important it is to make your practical interactions as businesslike as possible and to make your loving interactions as loving as possible. It's a huge time-saver.

So when you sit down to discuss a problem, do what you'd do at a meeting. Make sure there's an agenda with a goal attached to it: "We're sitting down to talk so that when we're done, we'll have a decision about whether we're going to buy a car this year or wait until next year." Then you have to stick to it.

I know what you're going to say: when you're in a relationship, every decision seems connected to every other decision. That's true. But paying too much attention to this is the route to paralysis. You'll feel an enormous sense of satisfaction if you stick to one issue at a time. That vastly increases your chance of coming away with a resolution.

The bonus is that when your practical interactions are more businesslike, your loving interactions will be more loving.

Chapter Sixteen

FEELING AT HOME
IN YOUR RELATIONSHIP

J immy had done something that's always very dangerous for people in a weekend marriage. He promised he'd take on a household project in his spare time—removing their old bathtub and putting in a Jacuzzi. You'd think it was something he could manage, since he was a plumber.

He did a good job removing the bathtub. It was fiberglass. No big deal. But somehow installing the Jacuzzi turned into the quest for the Holy Grail. And that was a big problem for his wife.

Sure, Nancy mostly took showers. But at least once a week she liked to recharge her batteries by having a nice long soak in the tub. For a while now Jimmy had been telling her that he didn't know when he'd be able to get around to putting in the Jacuzzi. It took time to find the right model at a big enough discount. He needed another guy to help him install it. He was tied up with other things.

After one more weekend went by during which Jimmy had promised to install it but hadn't, Nancy felt hurt and ignored and disrespected. So she lost it. She got really mad and started yelling at Jimmy. Deep down it was very innocent, though. She didn't want to punish him. She just wanted him to know how much this mattered to her.

But all Jimmy saw was an angry woman and all he heard was her yelling at him. All Nancy accomplished with her deep passionate feelings was Jimmy's responding, "Jeez, stop yelling." Nancy felt Jimmy hadn't heard a thing she'd said. It was incredibly discouraging. She felt as if every remaining bit of her positive energy had turned to negative energy.

But what can you do? People get mad, right?

Sure. But the question is, how much of this can you afford when you're living the weekend marriage. And what's the alternative?

Anger is basically feelings with the volume turned way up. But anger wastes a lot of time. Usually the volume is so loud that the other person can't hear the message, as if you turn up the stereo so loud that it sounds more like noise than music. Plus we say things to each other when we're angry that distort our message. With so much anger and so little time to talk in the weekend marriage, our need to feel heard is put in jeopardy. Still, we do need to feel heard.

In fact, our need to feel heard is what it's all about.

Here's a nightmare. You walk through the world but no one can see or hear you. You try to get their attention but they ignore you completely. If this kept up, first you'd get furious, then you'd panic, and then you'd be in despair.

This is a nightmare most of us have actually experienced in our waking life. There was the restaurant where you couldn't get the waiter's attention. The store where everyone acted as though you didn't exist. And for most of us there were plenty of times as kids when we were just hauled off for a day at some great-aunt's house and our protests were completely ignored.

We also experience a bit of this nightmare every day. At work, for example. Unless you're the big cheese, your needs and feelings as a human being are more irrelevant than you'd like. Who do you talk to about how scared you feel, or how incompetent sometimes?

We bring this sense of needing to feel heard and seen into our relationships. At some point in the early stages of our relationship, we had the experience of sharing something deeply personal about ourselves. And we found that we were accepted. This person we were falling in love with really heard us, and we loved them even more. Even better, they seemed to want to hear what we had to say.

This is one of the greatest gifts love brings us as individuals: *I hear you; I see you; your thoughts and feelings matter to me.*

This is deeply connected to our dream of a relationship filled with mutual honesty. What could possibly feel safer, warmer, more intimate than a relationship where you know you can say anything and it will be heard and accepted? And where you know your spouse won't keep anything from you? And where you feel confident you can accept everything your spouse says with love? This feels like the ultimate guarantee that you've found the one person in life who's right for you.

You *feel* you're in a mutually honest relationship when you're sure your spouse has really heard you about the issues and feelings that weigh on you, the burdens you carry in your heart, the things you think about in the middle of the night, the stuff you're longing to talk to someone about. That's when you achieve real intimacy. You've bared your soul and found acceptance. It's what we want from God. Just think how wonderful it is to get this from the man or woman you love.

But then the monster rises out of the weekend marriage to try to destroy this dream. You're feeling overloaded from your day. All kinds of important needs have gotten thrown overboard already. You feel as swamped by your life as a mouse on the *Titanic*. Then your spouse starts to complain. *No way!* You just can't let it in. You're not interested. It's too much. Besides, you've got a belly full of things to say yourself. (Remember Jimmy with the Jacuzzi? Didn't Nancy understand how hard he worked, how much he had on his mind, how touchy it was getting expensive plumbing fixtures at a discount?)

Maybe once you've gotten everything off your chest, you might be able to listen to your spouse, but when is there time for it?

Our dream of mutual honesty takes a hit when no one feels listened to. Does it make sense to say, *We can tell each other anything— we just can't listen to each other?* That's not honesty. It's noise.

Love promises many things, but one of its biggest, firmest promises is a sympathetic, open ear. So when we don't feel heard in our relationship, we feel betrayed as well as humiliated.

INSIGHT FOR ACTION

You won't feel at home in your relationship unless you're confident that your spouse really knows how you feel and understands your experiences. If you decide this is something you want, then take responsibility for getting it. Make sure you really do get heard and make sure you do it in a way that's respectful of your spouse.

This is important because there are so many issues people want to feel heard about.

You want to feel heard about grievances from the past—hurts, losses, disappointments. "I don't think you've ever appreciated how hurt I was when I found out that you slept with your old girlfriend after we'd been dating for a while." When someone carries this in her heart, she doesn't need to be told it was "nothing." There's not a single word in any language that you can use that will help her see that you understand how hurt she was. Only listening can do that. Not explaining, not defending. Just listening.

You want to feel heard about important needs you have right now that aren't being met. For example, "You say you have to spend so much time doing all the work you do, but you don't get how lonely I am, how difficult it is for me just waiting for you to come home, always hoping you'll be in a good mood, that we'll have some extra time together. But it never happens." Men and women want immediate solutions to real ongoing problems. But if the problems were easy to solve, you'd have solved them already. Until you find a solution, your spouse needs to know that you get what a big deal this problem is, that you understand what she needs and why she needs it.

You and your partner both want to feel heard about *whatever* is important to you, whether it's the environment or his father's deteriorating health or her investment portfolio or vacation plans or whatever: "Okay, so it looks like the promotion is going to go either to me or to Fred. I'm very nervous. I think everyone knows I've brought in more business than Fred. But he's so tight with the big boss. I know I should try to get closer to Mr. Philips, but I'm afraid he'll think that I'm just sucking up to him."

It can sometimes seem as though people go on forever about the stuff that runs through their heads. But how do you know there's no limit if you don't give him a chance? Maybe your spouse is talking a lot but not really saying what's most important. Do a test. Listen without interrupting. Draw your spouse out. Show that you *get it*. He'll probably stop going on and on once you've proven that you've really heard what he has to say.

But wait a minute, you might say, this is the weekend marriage we're talking about. We don't have time to listen to each other. How do we balance our need to feel heard with what I know our relationship needs, which is less stress? And that's a real problem for the weekend marriage. When two people are too eager to be heard about too many things, especially negative things, something's got to give.

Guerrilla tactics. Before you waste any time, wait and make sure your need to feel heard is more than just something that will pass. This is a revolutionary idea to some people, an unacceptable idea to others. *What? I have to watch what I say?* Well, you do if you want to have as much mutual honesty as possible while you're living the weekend marriage.

That's right: sometimes thinking for a minute before you talk actually promotes mutual honesty. When there's too much "negativity clutter"—too much of your negativity piled on top of your spouse's negativity piled on top of . . .—then no one has room to tell the important truths of their heart. You just have two frazzled people in reaction to one another. And you get negativity clutter when both spouses feel they have to get every pain and problem they've experienced off their chest.

Let's say you've had a really lousy day at work. On the drive home all you want to do is tell your spouse about how lousy your day was. Fine. But first ask yourself two questions. *If I don't get it off my chest about what a lousy day I had, will I explode?* And, *How do I feel about the fact that my spouse has probably had a lousy day, too—do we* both *need to take the time to complain about our lousy days?*

It's up to you. But realize you have a choice and realize the consequences of your choice for positive energy and mutual honesty in your relationship. Since getting rid of negativity is so important, I recommend you wait twenty-four hours if you have something you want your spouse to hear. If twenty-four hours later you still want to unburden yourself, it's a sign that it's really important to you to feel heard about this topic. You'd better make sure that you *do* end up feeling heard. If you don't, you'll end up feeling resentful.

Mutual honesty begins with your realizing that your honesty does you no good if you've not been heard. So the most important question isn't, *What is my truth?* but, *How do I present my truth so that I end up feeling heard?* Telling the truth without making sure that you've been heard is like throwing a party but forgetting to invite anybody.

And I have a promise I want to make to you. You can always make your spouse more receptive to hearing what you have to say. That's in your power: creating greater receptivity.

Weekend-marriage couples get into a very bad dynamic when it comes to expressing themselves. To understand this dynamic, let's go back to the early days of your relationship. There you were, sprawled on the couch. You've been hanging out together. There was a long silence. Suddenly you said, "Do you really like getting together with Joe and Grace? I just don't enjoy hanging out with them. Can we stop seeing them so much?"

Perfect, simple, clear communication. Your spouse got it immediately. He understood the problem and understood what you wanted. And because you were so calm and relaxed, it was easy for him to say, "Sure, no problem." Or, "Well, I really like them and Joe is my best friend, but sure we can spend less time with them than we have been."

Think of how different it is, though, when you're up to your eyeballs in the weekend marriage. Both of you are incredibly distracted and needy. So instead of saying, "Let's spend less time with Joe and Grace," you held on to your feelings for a long time because there was never a good moment to share them. But then your feelings built up and eventually you let loose with a long, loud howl of protest, showing all your pain and anger. You're really trying to convey the message, *See what a big deal this is to me. See what a big idiot you are if you don't give me what I want.*

But you're telling this to someone who's already stressed out. From his point of view, you're adding a stressful message to the stress he already has. His instinctive response isn't, *Let me figure out how can I do what she wants.* His response is, *I don't want to hear this and it's not fair that I have to deal with it.*

What adds to the stress is that you probably haven't kept your feelings a complete secret. Usually, there's been an ongoing battle. You've been fighting to get heard. Your spouse's been fighting to stop listening. "Haven't we been over this?" your spouse has said many times. Sure you've been over it, but you've never gotten to the bottom of it.

So instead of feeling heard, you carry on a kind of underground warfare in which you drop little digs and hints and comments about how hard you work. And that's not satisfying for anyone.

Almost every weekend-marriage couple I talked to said that there was too much negativity in their relationship. Complaints, worries, regrets, recriminations: "I should've [this]," "You should've [that]," "If only we'd [something else]."

Here's the paradox. There's too much of this negativity, but the solution isn't to say *shut up*. Unfortunately, that's what too many weekend-marriage couples do say in one way or another. But this negativity is really just a leaky, annoying way of asking to be heard.

There's only one solution. If you need to be heard, you need to be heard all the way. So make sure that's what you're asking for: "I want you to listen to how I feel about this." Now you've done something good. Instead of making a big mess, you've put forward one simple thing that you need.

So stay focused on what's bothering you and what you want your spouse to do about it. That's your truth. Now how do you communicate it so it gets through?

COMMUNICATING THE TRUTH is all about creating receptivity. This is something I'm very hopeful about. I truly believe that almost anyone can hear almost anything and let it in if who they are and what they need are taken into account. This means that you can be totally honest with your spouse and have him asking for more honesty, if you take him into account.

Think of it like this. If a cook said, "I believe in healthy food but I don't care if it looks appetizing," how would that be different from his trying to turn people off healthy food? You'd have to care about making healthy food look appetizing if you cared about people eating it.

So there you are with a need to be heard. How do you guarantee receptivity?

When you were a kid, you knew not to ask your parents for things when they were in a bad mood. Well, if you knew that much about receptivity when you were a kid, think of how good you can be at it now.

You can make your spouse incredibly receptive if you just think about who, what, why, when, and where.

Who. Who are you telling this to? This is a real person with real needs and real feelings. Maybe he's been feeling badly about himself recently. If so, he'll be much more receptive to your feedback if you couch it with a lot of support and praise. Maybe you know that he's not very talented at doing what you're asking. If so, your message has to be accompanied with a lot of encouragement and specific suggestions for how to do it.

I'll let you in on a secret. An important reason our spouses haven't been all that receptive to what we have to say is that we haven't given much thought to who they are. That's good news for you. You don't need to be a genius to do a great job. If you just try to think about who you're conveying your message to, the difference from what you were doing before will be so clear that your spouse will be much more receptive. He'll really feel that you're taking him into account.

What. What exactly are you saying? Yeah, I know—you're fed up, pissed off. You've had it. You can't believe your spouse is such a blankety-blank. *But is that actually your message?*

Remember: the message is the "take away"—what your spouse actually takes away from what you've said. I once saw a couple where the woman had gotten really upset about how her husband wasn't affectionate and romantic. In the course of haranguing him, she happened to mention, ". . . my friend Tracy's husband writes her little love notes. . . ." She'd just thrown this out as a tiny example of the kind of thing she was talking about. But that's what he glommed on to. His take away was, *I'd better write her little love notes.*

But that wasn't what she wanted her message to be. She wanted her message to be, *Be more affectionate and romantic when we're together. Be a little sexy and teasing and seductive when you talk to me.*

So do this. Imagine you've said whatever it is you have to say. The conversation's over. *What's the one thing you want your spouse to have in his head?* That's the take away. That's what you have to make sure you say in such a way that he hears it.

So suppose you're feeling like saying "Do you have any clue how irresponsible you are?" But suppose the message you want your spouse to take away is something like "Wow, I never realized how happy I would make her if I paid the bills on time, especially since I promised to do that."

Well, if that's what you'd like him to take away, then say that: "I'm so overloaded these days—how'd you like to make me really happy? Please, please pay all the bills the minute they come in so we don't fall behind and get in trouble. I can't tell you how much I'll appreciate that."

Don't you think your message will get through really well if it matches what you want your spouse to take away?

An extra tip. Talk about only *one issue at a time*. It's a mistake to try to be heard about more than one issue. I realize that everything is connected to everything else. But remember that your need is to feel heard. If you start piling one issue on top of another, at some point your partner will start feeling dumped on and he'll shut down, and you'll end up not feeling heard.

Why. One of the first things you forget when you're living the weekend marriage is that your spouse really loves you and wants to make you happy. You just don't see it, and why would you? You're both so under the gun that you can barely take care of your own needs, much less the other's. But let me ask you this. If you were in serious trouble, would your spouse drop everything? Of course. If not, you shouldn't be together.

You know how they say that you catch more flies with honey than you do with vinegar? Maybe if we trusted each other a little more, we'd put out more honey and catch more flies.

If your spouse has been putting up walls, maybe it's not because he doesn't care about you but because he doesn't appreciate why it's important to you. For example, why should you care that he lets the bills pile up? "Because then I stop trusting you and start resenting you. My feelings toward you turn sour. Then it's hard for me to want to get close to you."

This is incredibly helpful. Now your spouse knows what's at stake. It's not about your improving him. It's about your wanting to stay connected to him.

That's what it means to say why you're asking for something.

You're letting your partner know what the consequences are either way. You're not threatening or complaining. You're just describing how, realistically, when you don't get what you want, something bad happens, and you're showing him what that is. And you're describing how something good happens when you do get what you want. You're being clear about what's at stake. And you can make these points while you're being as cool as a cucumber.

When. You don't have to be a rocket scientist to figure out when your spouse is most receptive to what you have to say. It's not when he's tired, rushed, pissed off, or stressed out. It's not anytime it pops into your head to say it. I know there's rarely time in the weekend marriage, but some times are still better than others. Your spouse is most receptive when he's relatively relaxed, when the two of you have some time together, and when something good has either just happened or is about to happen.

This is not, for example, when you've just gone to bed. Bedtime is a bad time for serious discussions. Yes, your spouse may be relaxed, but he's tired, he's needing to stay relaxed, and he doesn't have time to talk because he's needing to get to sleep. And beware: weekend-marriage couples get into terrible messes when they stay up late talking about problems.

If you want to know when your spouse is most receptive, the best thing to do is to *ask him.* You might be surprised. It might be right after dinner. It might be anytime you're driving, as long as it's just the two of you and you're not rushing to get somewhere. It might be on the phone during the workday, although for other people that's the worst time.

Where. There are two places that are guaranteed to destroy your spouse's receptivity. One is any place where there's a lot of distraction. Like when the TV is on. Or when other people are around. The other kind of place that destroys receptivity is one in which your spouse will feel trapped if you pounce on him. Some people feel that way in cars. Your spouse might feel that way when he's in the bathroom. Just make sure that he doesn't feel cornered or distracted.

HERE'S WHAT ONE woman said who managed to bring her relationship back from the brink while she was living the weekend marriage. "I remember one Thursday evening. We'd both gotten home from work late. There was no food in the house. My husband and I got in this horrible fight. I don't remember what I said to him but it was obviously some huge putdown. And then I remember saying, hey, I'm just being honest. And he said, all right, let me be honest with you. And he said these really hurtful things. And I remember feeling, this can't be honesty. Honesty's not supposed to be like this. It's supposed to bring you closer, not be a way of attacking each other. What good is this so-called honesty if we can't hear each other?"

That's why receptivity is the key to mutual honesty. It guarantees that your truth will get through to the person who needs to hear it. You wouldn't send a package by wrapping it up and then dropping it in a hole in the ground. You'd drop it off at FedEx or UPS. Sure, you have to put a little bit of thought into receptivity. But then you're done. Your message gets through. You feel heard. And that takes a lot less time in the long run than endless arguments where no one hears anyone.

BEING HONEST AND communicating clearly is very different from what we call venting. I think that's a good word. It's as if these poisonous emotional gases have built up and you need to discharge them. But venting usually goes beyond just saying how you feel. Venting includes *showing* how you feel. It can get pretty intense.

Venting is like fire. It's a good thing, but it's very dangerous if it's not handled right.

Guerrilla tactics. If you want to save yourself from a big fat mess, let your spouse know that you need to vent. Say, "Listen, I'm really upset about something and I just need to vent. These are just my feelings. I don't want you to take everything I'm saying all that seriously. But I do need you to know how I feel."

Now, it can be pretty intense to listen to someone vent, too. So if it's a big enough deal for you to vent, then you should give your spouse a chance to say when he can listen to you and for how long. Then keep to that. If your spouse said three minutes, then stop after three minutes. That's a long time to hear someone yell at you about how he's sick of working so hard and yet you can never seem to save any money.

You can say whatever you want when you vent. The poisonous emotional gases are what they are. You can label, blame, threaten, curse, insult—you name it. It's okay. Your words are just feelings. They're not actions. They're nothing you'd sign your name to. You don't mean all the things you're saying but they're okay to say because they express your feelings. And because you've labeled it venting, you don't have to later apologize for saying stuff that you didn't really mean. That's what venting is.

Some people ask about the issue of verbal abuse. Verbal abuse is, of course, a real and large problem. Make no mistake. It can be as psychologically painful and destructive as physical abuse. But with venting you're protected because there are very specific rules about how to vent. And you both obey these rules because you want the other to obey them.

With venting, you label what you're doing as expressing feelings. "I just need to vent now. These are just feelings I have to get off my chest." Verbal abuse, on the other hand, comes across as if the person saying it were making a flat statement of reality.

With venting, you ask permission to let off steam: *"Is this a good time for you?"* If the other person says *no,* you don't vent. In verbal abuse, the person on the receiving end of it always feels ambushed and taken prisoner.

With venting, there's a time limit: "I can listen to you for two minutes." When the two minutes are up, that's that. This makes it safe for both of you. Verbal abuse tends to go on and on and you can't stop it.

With venting, there's a good intention. You want to let off steam so you're no longer choked by the noxious vapors of your own emotions. Once you've let off some steam, you can talk reasonably about underlying issues. With verbal abuse, the intention is to control the other person.

As long as you follow these rules, no one should feel verbally abused. You're both being empowered instead of one of you being disempowered.

One more thing about venting. It shouldn't happen very often when you're living the weekend marriage. Even when it's controlled, it's intensely negative. It's good that there's the occasional release, but if either one of you feels a frequent need to vent, then the first thing you have to do isn't to vent more but to check out how stress is causing frustration and conflict as you try to live your time-starved lives.

Chapter Seventeen

HOW TO LISTEN
TO SAVE TIME

People who cope just fine with the weekend marriage face the same dilemma everyone else does. They feel just as overloaded. They're just as hungry to be heard. So what do they do differently?

When it comes to feeling heard, a relationship is like a potluck dinner: there will be tons to eat, but for the price of admission you have to bring some food of your own. You have to cook for others before you can eat what others have cooked. And yet no one complains, "Those damn potluck dinners. That's how the bastards get you!" Instead, it feels great to chip in a little when you get back so much.

In the same way, in your relationship there will be plenty of opportunities for you to feel heard, but as the price of admission you have to do some listening of your own. I know I said that we're overloaded and our nerves are raw. It's true. But the main reason we don't listen isn't that we can't; it's because we've never

learned how. So there's way less mutual honesty in our relationship than we'd like because whatever it is we think we're doing,
we're still not really listening.

But we need to listen to each other. It's by listening that people tune in to love.

INSIGHT FOR ACTION

Listening is the art of helping the other person get emotionally naked. When someone shares a feeling, even if
it's negative, they're saying I want to strip off all the lev-
els until I've said everything there is to say *and* I stand
completely naked before you. People feel heard when
there's nothing left for them to say and when they're
confident you've gotten what they were trying to say.
Listening means helping them to do that.

But there's one more piece to this. People can't listen to you
until they feel you've heard them. That means that there you are
with your hunger to feel heard, but you just won't be able to satisfy it until you've made sure your spouse feels heard first.

I know what you're going to say. *What about me?* I understand.
This is one of the difficulties with the weekend marriage. You
have two people, little time, and both of you are hungry to feel
heard. And so you each raise the volume louder and louder and
still no one feels heard.

What about you? Well, we know that raising the volume hasn't
worked for you, right? It doesn't work for anyone. It just makes
you feel more angry and more deprived.

So think of it like this. If you both continue demanding to be heard, raising the volume, then maybe in a million years you might finally both get heard. But if you start listening to your spouse today, even though in some way it's not fair that you are the one to make the first move, your spouse might be able to listen to you tomorrow. Maybe even today, if you do a really good job of listening yourself.

Here's what listening to someone *isn't*. It isn't a tribunal. It isn't about establishing who's right. Listening is about your spouse feeling heard, period. Sorting out the truth can come later. So when you listen to him and he says things that are untrue, unfair, unrealistic, unconscionable, even insane, and every ounce of you is wanting to correct this or that flagrant error, you can't give in to that impulse. Because then you're back in the old shouting match where you have two people talking and no one feels heard.

I'll be blunt. If your spouse is not a basically fair person, someone who can appreciate evidence and eventually let in someone else's point of view, then you should get out of that relationship. You're married to a power person, someone who just wants to win. But don't confuse someone who just wants to win with someone who just wants to feel heard. There's a big difference, although they can sound the same when a person is very frustrated. The difference is that if your spouse is basically fair, then once she feels heard, she'll be able to see your point of view.

Here are the secrets of successful listening.

Just listen. Sitting there with your mouth closed and your ears open, especially when you hear things that make you want to jump up and say *No!* will help your spouse feel you really want to hear what she has to say. People often ask, "Well, when I'm listening, why can't I also doodle, chop onions, balance my check-book, fold the laundry, and take the toaster apart?" I understand. Some people are just fidgeters, like my husband. Some people are uncomfortable listening to emotional outpourings. Some people have gotten in the habit of not making eye contact when they listen.

All I can do is tell you the truth. When you're not just sit-ting quietly looking at the person who's talking to you, she's going to be wondering, *Are you listening? Can you hear me?* She'll talk louder, longer, and more dramatically just to make sure you hear her.

If you want to save time, sit quietly and listen.

Ask questions. You should be quiet when you listen except when it comes to asking questions, and you should ask tons of questions. They should all be questions designed to bring out more of what's inside your spouse. It's hard to say what questions you should ask because it all depends on the situation. But you should probably ask questions like:

> *How long have you felt this way?*
> *Why is this so important to you?*
> *What other feelings is this connected to?*
> *What was it like for you?*
> *What's been my role in this as you see it?*
> *What started this?*
> *What do you need?*
> *How can I help?*
> *What's the next step?*

Now you might be reluctant to ask questions because you're fed up with all the negativity and this just seems like a crazy way to bring more negativity down on your head. But this is really a way to put an end to a preexisting lump of negativity that won't disappear any other way.

Remember: most negativity isn't an expression of a negative feeling. It's an expression of not feeling heard about a negative feeling. Your spouse, for example, doesn't get all snarly about how "you haven't been there for me" because you haven't been there for him. The snarly part comes because he doesn't feel you've heard the hints he's dropped for how you haven't been there for him. It's your listening that makes the negativity go away.

The art of asking questions so the other person feels he's getting to tell his story depends on your not coming across like a trial lawyer playing gotcha. Instead, you need to come across like someone who wants to appreciate every facet of the story your spouse has to tell.

I call this *unpacking the bag*. Imagine your spouse has handed you a travel bag. You unzip it and there you see a layer of stuff on the surface. But you go further. If you want to see everything in the bag, then you take out each item, one at a time, and really examine it until there's nothing left in the bag to examine.

This is how to make your spouse feel really listened to. You unpack the bag of her story or her feelings. And you do it by asking questions that bring out everything inside. And you need to hang in there asking more and more questions. Remember, all the really interesting stuff is going to be on the bottom, and it's only your hanging in there really listening that will make them feel safe enough to share the stuff on the bottom.

And you never know you've reached the bottom until your spouse has nothing left to say.

Keep yourself out of it. The act of listening to someone is not about you. Even if your spouse's words are all about you, listen with the kind of interest you'd show if you were your spouse's best friend. People are hungry for their spouse to be their best friend, someone they can unburden themselves to who won't react to what they've just heard. And *you can do that.* Just don't be in reaction. Don't respond as if you were being attacked, even if the words are all about things you've done wrong. In truth, you really aren't being attacked. Yes, your spouse has some negative feelings. Yes, they're largely about you. But her *need* is to feel heard. And you can only satisfy her need by listening. By the way, the fact that you just listen and don't argue back doesn't mean that you're agreeing with the content of what your spouse is saying. Don't worry. You'll get your turn.

Make little comments to show that you're listening. If a friend of yours was talking about some disaster she'd gone through, you might say, "Wow, that's really terrible." A comment like this is just a way of saying, "I hear you." You're showing that you notice what the other person has said. Or you might say, "You mean while you were going through that you didn't feel you had anyone you could talk to? You must've felt so lonely." There's no magic involved in reflecting back what you've heard. Just listen, and say what you've understood. But no editorializing. You're trying to make sure that your spouse doesn't feel like she's talking to a wall.

Keep listening until your spouse has nothing more to say. How will you know that your spouse "feels heard"? Ask. "Do you feel you've been heard?" You want to hear him say something like "I feel you've finally heard me." This will take less time than you think. More important, it will take less time than the alternative, which is the endless time-eating battle where one of you keeps fighting to be heard and the other tries to shut her up.

Say what you've understood. Here's a very common and very bad way people in relationships try to show that they've heard their spouse. They say, "Yes, but . . ." That single word *yes* is designed to signal that they've heard everything. But then with the word *but* they're launched into explaining their own side of the story. In fact, though, saying "Yes, but . . ." signals that they've heard nothing and don't care about hearing anything.

It's only by summing up that you provide real evidence that you've gotten what your spouse's been saying and taken it in.

Let's say there are constant negativity leaks into your relationship because your spouse feels you "weren't there for me" when she was pregnant. So she keeps on telling you about it, over and over. But your spouse does that because she feels that you've never understood how she feels about this, because every time she brings it up, you defend yourself. She starts complaining and then you say "Yes, but . . ." and then launch into an explanation of how you really were there for her (which tells her that she must be crazy for feeling the way she does) or into an explanation of how hard you tried to be there for her (and that just makes you seem lame).

Here's the deal. Every thirty seconds you spend contradicting, explaining, deflecting, doing anything but listening creates thirty *minutes* of more talk and more negativity. So you have to do it differently. You say, "I really want to hear how you feel about my not being there for you when you were pregnant." Then you listen, listen, listen. You ask questions and "unpack the suitcase."

Then comes the crucial step. You repeat back to her a brief, summary version of the essential points of what she's said. It's really easy to do this. If you were listening, you'll get it. Just make sure you focus on how she feels, and why. You could say something like "I think I really get it this time. The whole time you were pregnant, I was working so hard and I'd always come home late and be exhausted. You were basically alone that whole time and you felt very lonely. I never went to your doctor's appointments with you. You felt abandoned. And when you'd complain about how lousy you felt, I'd tell you to tell your doctor, not me, and I'd make you feel like you were being a baby for complaining. Here was this huge event that was supposed to bring us closer, and it drove us apart. I was never there for you. And then when you got big and felt you were ugly, it seemed like I was rejecting you."

If your partner feels you've left out or distorted some important point, that's okay. Just say back what you've understood after you've been corrected.

And most of all, DO NOT use this as an opportunity to defend yourself or explain what you were doing. Yes, from your point of view, you were certainly not intending to abandon your spouse. You were just working as hard as you possibly could to bring in money because you guys really needed it, especially since your wife would soon have to stop working for a while. And yes, you'd never witnessed a pregnancy before and you felt completely inadequate. But this is not the time for defenses or explanation.

I know this might sound crazy. You might feel it's practically an admission of guilt not to defend yourself. But you can't think about that now. You will never get a hearing yourself until your spouse feels heard. But the good news is that *once* your spouse really does feel heard, you'll be surprised at how little interest she'll show in continuing to rake you over the coals. In a court of law the issue is decided by the weight of the evidence. In the weekend marriage the issue is put behind you by your showing that you've really listened. People in the weekend marriage want a hearing, not a trial.

Weekend-marriage couples sometimes feel that this kind of extended, careful, thorough listening session is a big fat waste of time. I understand. It's kind of paradoxical: there you are in a world without time where what you want to do is communicate in sound bites, but what you really *need* is to stop time and unpack the bag. When time is short, there are tradeoffs. You obviously don't have the time to spend hours listening to each other. But when you're thinking about what to do with the limited time available to you, listening is just about the best investment you can make.

My personal rule of thumb is that at least 70 percent of what your spouse does that you find obnoxious grows out of his not feeling heard. Something good happens to people when they get to the point where they feel heard all the way down to their toes. They soften. They seem much less demanding. They're more open to what you have to say. They're more generous. They're less wordy.

If you're going to make sure that you have more of the good stuff and less of the bad stuff in your weekend marriage, radical listening like this is a great place to start.

Show that you're sorry. The basic message you want to convey is *I'm so sorry you went through what you did. I'm so sorry you had those experiences. I'm so sorry you had those feelings. I'm so sorry for my part in all this. I'm so sorry I haven't really heard you about this before.* Now don't confuse this with groveling or eating dirt or taking blame for something you didn't do.

Look, if you went to a funeral, you'd go up to the bereaved and say, "I'm so sorry for your loss." You're not saying you killed the guy. You're just sorry for the fact that he's dead.

But in our relationship, we withhold a sincere expression of how sorry we are because we're more interested in justifying our own behavior or avoiding accusations. Or else we say *I'm sorry* in a perfunctory way (as in "I *said* I'm sorry, didn't I?"). And then *I'm sorry* really means *I wish you'd shut up.* My advice: don't worry about incriminating yourself. It's not about that. It's about this: if something bad happened to me, then I don't feel you've understood until you feel bad about what happened to me.

You have no idea how much time all this saves. Based on my analysis of couples' interactions, at least 50 percent of negative interactions are related to grievances from the past about which people don't feel heard. Weekend marriages are suffering from a kind of Chinese water torture that comes from unfinished business. Because your spouse doesn't feel that you've really heard her about some problem, she keeps mentioning it and mentioning it and mentioning it—drop, drop, drop—until you feel that all she's done is talk about it and she feels that you've never heard a word of what she has to say about it. The torture stops when your spouse feels heard.

So what felt as though it was endlessly unresolved wasn't unresolvable. It's just that no one had taken the time to really sit down and make sincere efforts to demonstrate how sorry they were.

Find out what, if anything, you need to do to rebalance things. We live in a very litigious society, and so many of our instincts are organized around avoiding responsibility because we want to protect ourselves. Just check out how many courtroom shows there are. *Court TV, The People's Court, Judge Judy, Judge Hatchett, Judge This, Judge That.* We're told to take responsibility for ourselves, but the message of this courtroom society is to do everything possible to avoid being held responsible.

In marriage, you have to take responsibility. So after you've really, truly heard what your spouse has to say and you've expressed how sorry you are, *ask what you can do to rebalance things.* Again, it's not about whether you're guilty. It's about showing your love and trying to take care of each other. If something was hard for your spouse in the past, ask how you can make things easier for her in the future. If your spouse was deprived of something in the past, ask how you can make it up to her in the future.

We never have a stronger sense that we've been heard than when we're given hope that our future will be better.

Chapter Eighteen

HOW TO NEVER GET STUCK AGAIN

"*Every time a problem comes up,*" Miriam said, "*even if we don't mean to be negative, Joe and I start talking and I think we're intending to be constructive, but it turns into such a mess so fast. I can never figure out how it happens. But it sure ends up feeling a lot more negative and confusing than we wanted it to be.*"

Ahh, the mess. Every couple knows about this. Maybe you call it the tangle. Maybe it feels like getting caught in spiderwebs. Some couples refer to it as getting caught in quicksand.

The weekend marriage is about saving your love when you don't have much time. And that means eliminating all the interactions from your relationship that you'll just have to clean up later—those long, messy, painful conversations where you really don't know what you're talking about, why you're talking about it, where you're headed, and how this mess got started in the first place. All you know is that you'd rather be pulling splinters of glass out of your knee than doing this, but you just don't know how to stop. You start talking and, damn it, it should've been so easy and simple—so how did you end up in this big, complicated, confusing fight? It seems like such a mystery.

This is one mystery I can solve.

INSIGHT FOR ACTION

There are three things people do when they talk. Two are good: they say how they feel, or they ask for what they need. The other usually causes problems all by itself: they define reality. Couples get into terrible trouble when they mush these three together. Nothing gets settled and no one feels satisfied. And this is seriously aggravated when you have very little time.

Here's how to prevent the mess.

There are two good things you can do when you have a problem. You can do either one, but you can do only one at a time. Sorry to be so strict, but I'm just telling it like it is, especially when you're caught up in the pressure of the weekend marriage. As you'll see in a moment, when you mix these two things up, you instantly descend into a painful mess.

ONE OF THE two good things you can do is *say how you feel.* Saying how you feel means nothing more than describing your feelings in words. *I'm angry; I'm sad; I'm scared; I'm happy; I'm grief stricken; I'm relieved; I'm overwhelmed; I'm proud; I'm tired; I'm looking forward to . . .* You get the point. It's exactly what you want to do when you want to vent, when you want to be heard, when you want your spouse to know how important something is to you, when you want to break down a barrier of distance and misunderstanding by sharing how you feel. When you want to get close. It's mutual honesty in action.

Saying how you feel shouldn't be used to do anything else. It particularly shouldn't be used to negotiate the tricky waters of getting your spouse to meet some need of yours. Why? Because then it won't be clear what's going on and you'll end up in a mess. You can *feel like* walking out of your relationship because you're so frustrated even though that's the last thing you'd actually do. Things will get complicated and confused between you, because strong feelings give a very confusing picture of what you really need.

Emotions are not the problem. Confusion is the problem. As long as it's clear that you're saying only how you feel, you'll avoid a mess.

Suppose you vent for a couple of minutes about how *I've been so mad recently. I feel I have all the responsibility for everything. I'm exhausted. I don't think it's fair the way we've arranged things. I feel so frustrated and overwhelmed.* You're doing one thing and one thing only: letting your spouse know how you feel. You're not asking for something. You're just saying how you feel, which means you'll be happy simply if he hears you.

You have to be careful. If you start throwing around demands when you say how you feel, take it from me, you'll end up doubly frustrated because your spouse won't really hear your demands. He'll just hear complaints. Plus, when you're upset, you'll start piling on unrelated demands and that will just make things more confused and waste more time.

And remember, if you're listening to someone say how they feel, all you have to do is give a clear indication that you've heard their feelings and understood them. Then, if you want, you can join them and talk about how you've felt similarly. Or share whatever feelings you have.

I said there were two good things you can do when a problem comes up. Saying how you feel was one. Here's the other one.

You can say what you need. For some reason, the idea of having needs in a relationship has gotten a bad reputation. But people confuse having needs with being needy. *Needy* means that you have too many needs and that your needs are too big for anyone and you put too much of your energy trying to get your spouse to meet these needs.

But the idea that you don't have any needs is nuts. To be alive is to have needs. You need your spouse not to hog all the blankets at night. You need your spouse to give you fifteen minutes to unwind, for chrissake, when you come home. You need physical affection. You need respect. Why in the world would we ever get married if it weren't for the fact that we have needs that can best be met by this person?

When you're living the weekend marriage, your needs become even more important. Your time is in such short supply that you've already dumped a lot of your needs. There've been days when you look ahead at your hectic schedule and you say *I'm not going to get any quiet time to myself today. I'm not going to be able to go out for lunch. I'm not going to be able to watch my favorite show on TV.* So when you have a need that you can bring to your spouse, a lot rides on your being able to express your need in a way that will ensure that it gets met.

To ensure your need will get met, saying how you feel is *not* a good idea. It's just a way to vent. Now I understand that it's a bummer to hear that you have to keep needs and feelings separate. You just want to relax and let the words tumble out of your mouth. I felt that way myself for years. I didn't want to talk if I couldn't do it in a completely free way. But the price I paid was getting into huge messes with my husband where the intensity of my feelings distracted him from dealing with my needs and my list of needs made it hard for him to hear my feelings. Don't worry about keeping your feelings and needs separate if tangled, messy, time-consuming conversations with your partner aren't a problem. But if the mess is a problem, then you have to keep them separate.

Now if you listen to someone vent, you can often make a good guess about what they need. But one of the reasons we get into a big mess when we talk is that like a drunk driver we veer back and forth from the operatic emotionality of how we feel to the practical details of what we need.

Our spouses quickly get out of sync with us. You've let your partner know how you feel in spades. When you start talking about what you need, she's just beginning to digest what you've said about how you feel. And that's what she responds to, your feelings, not your needs. And if she's like most spouses, she talks about how you shouldn't get so upset. She's talking about your feelings, because that's where she's stuck. But you've moved on to talking about needs and so you think she's telling you that your needs aren't so important. You can see how this creates a mess.

Now, we've become so used to the mess that often no one thinks twice about it. Doesn't everyone have long, painful, confusing conversations that never really resolve anything? Yes, but so what? Galley slaves got used to being whipped all day but no one thinks that was a good way to live.

Weekend-marriage couples get divorced because they get

stuck in the mess and rarely have anything but useless, annoying conversations.

And ending the mess begins when you make a decision. *I can talk about how I feel. Or I can talk about what I need.* You can do whichever one you want. You can even do both. But never at the same time. And never without labeling which one you're doing.

Here's a good example of saying what you need: "I need you to start getting dinner ready if you get home before me." You're putting forward one specific need of yours. It's fine to say why your need is important to you. But don't confuse that with an intense expression of emotion. Saying why your need is important to you is a matter of giving clear information. The calmer you are, the more easily your spouse will let in that information. "I've worked hard, it's been a long day, I'm hungry, and it's only fair that if you're home earlier, you'll start dinner."

Let's say your spouse has been spending too much money. You can talk about how upset you are about your spouse's overspending. *Or* you can have a discussion about how to rearrange your finances. But let me ask you this. How receptive do you think your spouse is going to be to a discussion about her cutting up her credit cards if you've just yelled at her?

I know what you think. *She just doesn't get it about the need to live within a budget.* So naturally you think you have to let her know how important this is, and what better way is there to convey the importance of this issue than to get emotional? But your own experience has shown you that it just doesn't work like this. When you turn up the volume, your spouse just hears noise. You think you're conveying, *This is important to me.* What you're actually conveying is, *Look at me—I'm a big, scary, angry person.*

Look, I can't tell you what to do. All I can do is pass on to you the lessons of people who've learned to keep their love alive in this time-starved world. And they've learned that if you have a need and want to get it met, the best thing to do is state that need simply, calmly, and directly.

And all you have to do when someone says what they need is for the two of you to put your heads together and figure out a way to meet that need.

These then are the two *good* kinds of couple talk, either saying how you feel or saying what you need, as long as you keep them separate.

There's another way couples get into terrible messes when they talk. Instead of talking about how they feel and what they need at the same time, *they talk about what's "real."*

Now obviously I'm not talking about sharing information, as in "I just heard the Smiths down the street put their house on the market and they're asking a lot of money for it." I'm talking about getting into arguments about what's real with your spouse.

These start, for example, when you make a pronouncement about who said what: "You said we were going to buy a house the minute you got your promotion." Then he says, "No, I said I'd think about our buying a house when I got my promotion." Who did what: "You were rude to my mother." Then she says, "No, I couldn't have been nicer." Who intended what: "You said that just to hurt my feelings." Then he says, "No, I was just telling the truth." And so on.

It seems so innocent. But it almost always leads to disaster. Suppose you say to your spouse, *"You deliberately wait for me to remind you to take out the garbage."* Of course you know that's true. Any idiot could see it. And how wonderful it would be if your spouse said, "My God, you're right. I do deliberately wait for you to remind me. Thanks for pointing it out." The only problem is that very few people in the entire history of the world have ever responded like this.

And that's the problem with talking about what's real. Yes, every once in a while you get agreement: "I saw you flirting with that woman at the party," she said. "Well, yeah, but I didn't think you'd mind," he said. But nine times out of ten, couples can never agree on what's real. In reality he'd say, "What are you talking about? I wasn't flirting. I was just being friendly. Your problem is that you can't tell the difference between someone flirting and someone being friendly." Uh oh—another statement about what's real leading almost certainly to another disagreement.

You can see how this leads to huge messes. You have some innocent need you want to talk to your spouse about: "I need you to take out the garbage without my reminding you." Or, "I need you not to flirt with women at parties." And the next thing you know, you're having a big fight about what's real, but fights about what's real can never be resolved because there's never anyone who can pull out a DVD, pop it in the player, and end the argument right there because the deed was caught on camera.

Instead, the fight spirals into a discussion of motives and biases— "You just want to control me." "You always think the worst of me."—that leave you feeling alienated and despairing.

It gets even worse when you fold in a discussion of what's real with talking about how you feel and what you need. Then these three things tumble over each other like three wildcats in a burlap bag. You don't know what you're saying. You don't know what you're talking about. You don't know where you're headed. You're just tumbling around in a nightmare of confusion. When you're living the weekend marriage, you don't have the time for messy fights that are so confusing you'll never figure out how to resolve them.

Here's my advice. Save time and save wear and tear on your relationship by always bypassing any discussion about what's real. The easiest thing is to just agree to disagree and go right to *"Look, just tell me what you want me to do."*

The only thing you can say that's real and true that no one can argue with is how you feel. On that you're the world's foremost expert! Beyond that, though, you're in dangerous water.

You can take a shot if you want: "Every night when you get home you collapse in your chair like you're completely exhausted." Maybe this will be one of those rare times where your spouse agrees. But if not, drop it and go right to either saying how you feel or asking for what you need. You're starved for time these days—why use the little time you have in pointless arguments?

The cool thing is that you don't need to agree about what's real in order to get your needs met. You'll see that you can work out beautiful solutions without any reference to motives, what happened in the past, who did what to whom first and when, what things really meant, or any other aspect of reality. Who cares if your husband says, "I was going to take out the garbage anyway"? Forget the past. Focus on the future and say what you need: "From now on, please put out the garbage right after dinner on Wednesday nights, so I don't have to spend the whole evening wondering if I'm going to have to remind you."

Guerrilla tactics. Successful weekend-marriage couples always deal with one another as if they are partners helping each other go through a difficult time together. This supports the idea that neither of you is the monster. The monster lives in the ways you get in trouble in a time-starved environment. And the monster loves to see the two of you getting into a big old mess when, under the pressure of time, you start lumping together talking about how you feel and what you need and what's real.

Be partners in fighting the monster by pointing out to each other when one of you sees the other starting to do this. Be gentle. You can say something like "I see you're upset about this. Just so we don't get all tangled up, what do you want to do? I'm happy to listen to your feelings. But if you want to tell me what you need and work out a solution with me, I'm happy to do that, too. But don't you think we want to keep them separate?"

Or you can say something like "Look, I think we're both starting to define reality for each other. We know where that usually gets us. We just don't see it the same way. But we don't need to if we just want to figure out what we're going to do from now on."

This is not disempowering you. This is empowering you to get what you want and at the same time protect the positive energy you have for each other.

Chapter Nineteen

WHAT ABOUT THE KIDS?

L et's face it, if romance were a disease, kids would be the cure. So if you want romance, you can't always let kids have their way.

Here's a little scene that has never happened in the entire history of the world, and never will.

PARENT: I hope you appreciate the fact that your parents sacrificed their relationship so we could play Boggle with you and help you with your science homework.

CHILD: Yes. I'm well aware of your sacrifice and I appreciate it very much. The fact that you guys are divorced now was a small price to pay for those golden moments.

You get the point. If you shortchange your relationship for the sake of your children, they won't appreciate it and might end up without a relationship as well.

Not everyone gets this point. Here's the kind of thing I've heard countless weekend-marriage couples say: "You have to sacrifice everything for your kids. That's the deal once you have kids. You have to give everything to them. But if you have a happy family life, your relationship will be there waiting for you when your kids are older and don't need you so much."

These couples think they're describing how things really work. But they're just offering up an attitude.

But I can tell you what successful weekend-marriage couples typically say. It's something quite different: "In this crazy, busy world we live in, everyone gets short shrift. Yes, there's a certain minimum amount of time kids need to feel loved, to feel part of their parents' lives. But it's less than you might think. Beyond that, if we parents sacrifice our relationship for our kids, we'll end up in divorce court. And that does no one any good. The best thing you can do for your child is to have a good marriage."

The secret is balance and a sense of priorities. Children make intimacy hard for couples living the weekend marriage. Prepare to fight for time for your relationship when you have kids.

INSIGHT FOR ACTION

A happy marriage is the foundation of a happy family. All the kid-centered time in the world won't seem as though it matters much if a couple gets divorced because their lack of time together killed their marriage.

Here's how to put this into practice.

Dump the guilt. Time spent strengthening your relationship isn't something to feel guilty about. On the contrary, it's a duty to the health of your marriage and your family. What do kids know?

They treat your time the way they do every junk item they see when you take them to the supermarket. They want more than they need. More than is good for them. More than will make them happy. They will drain your time like a vampire draining blood, but it won't make them happy.

It won't make them healthy either. It's not as if parents were some kind of vitamin P you could pour down their gullets—the more the better. As with other vitamins, a little vitamin P goes a long way. Here's something that *is* very healthy: your kid's being able to say, "My parents had a great marriage." Seeing the two of you giving to each other, getting along, working things out, showing you love each other is far more healthful to kids than most people realize. That's because your kid will be saying, "I want one of those for myself one day," and you've shown him what he needs to make it happen.

Think quality time, not quantity time. One of the greatest gifts you can give a child is your undivided attention. More important than how long your kid gets your undivided attention is letting your kid be in charge of what happens. They have ideas of what they need. Even an eighteen-month-old will let you know quite clearly how he wants to spend his time with you. If you're not sure, and if your child's old enough, ask what he wants. When you focus on your kid and his needs, and do things with him that he wants, you're giving him everything necessary for his optimal development, and it doesn't have to soak up all your time.

Junk time is good for you and your kids. I've talked about how it can be bad for your relationship with your spouse to use your precious time together in what I call junk time—washing dishes, straightening up, and so on. Unless you're very much in sync, this can be more a source of stress than an opportunity for closeness.

But this works very differently when it comes to your kids. Doing dishes and other chores with your kids can be good for them and good for your relationship with them. They often work harder when they're supervised. They don't feel you're intruding too much. And there are plenty of opportunities for them to bring up topics that have been on their mind.

Put a lid on the nagging, complaining, negativity. I know, I know. Your kids need a lot of improvement. Believe me, my kids do, too. What the heck, my mother still thinks I need a lot of improvement! But particularly when they're growing, it's easy for a parent to look at her six- or ten- or fourteen-year-old and think that he or she would benefit from nothing but nagging, correcting, and criticizing.

But the weekend marriage changes everything. The question you have to ask yourself is, *What percent of the little time you have with your kid do you want to spend nagging and criticizing?* Now here are two facts for you. You can believe them or not. All I can say is that I know them to be true based on my clinical and research experience.

- *Fact 1: The more time you spend nagging and criticizing your kid, the more it becomes an indelible part of his memory of what it was like to grow up as your child.* Please benefit from my professional experience. I can't tell you how many people have told me that what they remember most from their childhood was how their mother or father was on their back all the time. Now your not having much time with your kid means that you could spend twenty minutes nagging and criticizing and the next thing you know that's pretty much all the one-on-one time you have with him that day. We are responsible for our kids' memories of what it was like to grow up under our roof. I strongly believe that no more than 10 percent of your interactions with your kid should be taken up with nagging and criticism.

- *Fact 2: Most of the nagging and criticizing you do doesn't have much positive impact.* Here are the most important factors in determining the kind of adult a kid turns into. Most important: who he is, the stuff he was born with. And your actions have no impact on his fundamental personality. Next most important: who you and your spouse are. This includes how you live, how you talk, what's important to you, everything about the way you do things. Now here's the neat part. If you spend a lot of time keeping things clean because that's the way you like them, for example, your kid will probably want to live in a clean house when he's an adult. If you're ambitious and hardworking, your kid will probably be that way too.

You get the point. Between who your kid is and who you are, right there you have most of what's actually responsible for how your kid turns out. Criticizing and nagging don't add to this.

I know parents. You're going to do what you feel you need to do to take care of your kid and relieve yourself of the guilt that comes from not doing everything possible. I accept that. I'm just saying that if you want to enjoy your kid and still know you're doing a great job as a parent, you can take comfort from the fact that he'll still probably turn out just fine without your constantly being on his case. What do you think, that those parents who spend their time nagging and criticizing have kids who turn out great?

Don't confuse this with being involved with your kid. Parental involvement is definitely associated with what kids achieve. But parents who are successfully involved with their kids don't get sucked into nagging and criticizing once they see what's really going on after they've gotten involved.

Listen; don't micromanage. The key to being involved in a way that helps your kid but doesn't absorb all your precious time is to shift from micromanaging to listening. Micromanaging makes kids helpless. It gives them the message that they can't do it without you. It's not like training wheels. It's like getting your kid addicted to training wheels.

But your listening to your kid gives him the sense that *My life is my responsibility and that's okay. I can deal with it because I'm not alone.* Your listening makes your kid less helpless and enables him to think of you as a resource. It's not like training wheels. It's like you're nurturing your kid's inner balance so he doesn't need training wheels.

Besides, listening takes way less time than micromanaging.

Chapter Twenty

MANAGING MONEY
TO CREATE MORE TIME
FOR LOVE

There's been lots of research on what makes people truly happy. One of the findings that's been verified over and over is that to be happy you don't need tons of money. You just need enough to be able to pay your bills at the level of a middle-class lifestyle. Beyond that amount, more money doesn't result in a significant and lasting increase in happiness. For example, research has amply demonstrated that people who win huge lottery prizes are happier for only about six months (about the length of their spending spree), after which their level of happiness falls back to what it was before they won.

But love *does* make you happy.

So isn't it stupid to let fighting about money damage your love?

The fighting comes from the fact that most couples don't actually fit all that well together when it comes to dealing with money. After all, who falls in love with someone because of the way they handle money? How many people get married even knowing how their spouse handles money?

So no wonder there are so many money fights in the weekend marriage.

INSIGHT FOR ACTION

Nothing destroys positive energy faster than talking about money. But you can deal with money in such a way that you're more responsible and spend less time talking about it. This creates positive energy.

The best advice I can think of when it comes to money for weekend-marriage couples is to try to inherit a billion dollars. Although it won't guarantee happiness, it will sure save you a lot of nickel-and-dime discussions. But obviously for most of us weekend-marriage couples, this is not an option.

So let me give you the next best advice. Here's the **guerrilla tactic.** Set up your lives to minimize money talk and you'll minimize money fights. Here are some ways to do that.

The key to it all is keeping your money separate as much as possible. Couples get confused here because of misty-eyed ideology about "our money" and "sharing" and "trust." But that ideology will be of little comfort when you're mired in yet another conversation about how you spend this money.

Instead, have a clear agreement about who pays for what. Have it be proportional to your incomes. For example, if you earn roughly the same amount of money, then maybe one of you pays the mortgage and the other pays the other bills if they add up to pretty much the same amount. What some savvy weekend-marriage couples do is have one pay all the bills, and the other's paycheck goes into their retirement and savings accounts.

If one of you earns most of the money, he should give the other a regular sum that goes into her own separate checking account, just like a paycheck. It's humiliating to always have to come to your spouse and ask for money.

Never have a joint checking account—in my experience joint accounts take up hours of conversation a month.

Designate the most responsible one of you to actually pay the bills. Even if the most responsible one works more hours on a job, you'll still save time and money talk if that's the one who pays the bills. (You can rebalance the unfairness in other ways.)

You can also minimize money talk by setting budgets. If, for example, you've allocated a certain amount per month for clothing for each of you, then you can spend what you want when you want as long as you don't go over your budget. No muss, no fuss. But you have to keep to your budget. Going over budget is no joke. In my experience, budget busters are marriage busters.

Live as modestly as you can. Your expenses should be such that you can pay all your bills and still save some money. If your expenses don't allow that, then change the way you live so your expenses are lower.

I can't put it more bluntly than this. Couples who have trouble making ends meet or who are consistently racking up debt find that the positive energy is sucked right out of their relationship, to say nothing of the time they spend arguing and worrying over money. I understand that some big expenses, like housing, can't be cut down overnight. But I'm telling it like it is. People who "need" to have a certain lifestyle that they can't easily afford end up sacrificing their marriage to get it. Then guess how expensive divorce is!

When you do need to have money conversations, just use the tools in this part of the book. Make sure you listen. Don't confuse expressing your feelings about your money issue with saying what you need. Don't get bogged down in fights over who spent how much on what. And when you need to make a decision, say what you need (but don't try to talk each other out of your needs), kick the issue around for a while exploring possibilities, and then have one of you draft a solution. Tinker with it if you have to.

And remember that in no part of your relationship is following through on an agreement more important than when it comes to money.

MARRIED COUPLES NEED to have the sense that they belong together. This means that their fit is right. Maybe not perfect, but plenty good enough. You deserve that sense. But when it comes to the weekend marriage, money is just one of the areas where couples can find that they don't seem to fit all that well together. This makes them doubt whether they belong together in the first place.

And I think this doubt is usually a mistake. You probably do belong together, just not when it comes to money or some of the other areas where weekend-marriage couples get stuck. Anyway, weekend-marriage couples are successful because of all the things they do (and you've seen them in this book) that help them bridge their lack of fit.

Let's look at how all of this works.

It's the things people do when they're dating that cause them to fall in love with each other. So, for example, let's say part of the reason two people fell in love and got married was how much they both loved skiing, or how much they both loved lakes and hated the ocean. Or how much they both enjoyed going antiquing. Or how they had similar political or religious views. Or how good their sexual chemistry was. Or how quite simply they could lie in bed or drive in the car for hours and never run out of things to talk about, or never mind being silent together.

This means that in most cases we've selected our mates based on how well we fit together when we're having fun and hanging out, not based on how well we fit together when we come home late from work and we're tired and there's lots to do and not enough time to do it in. So when you and the love of your life face the practical challenges of the weekend marriage, you may be no better suited for each other than two people selected at random off the street.

All this is actually good news. It's no surprise that you don't have a great fit when it comes to your crunch-time interactions. *What! You didn't pay the electric bill? Why do you always put off paying bills? I can't believe there's anybody who doesn't know that you pay a bill the minute you get it.*

The real news flash here is something it's important to keep reminding yourself of: there was a reason why you got together with your spouse in the first place. It just felt right. You sensed a deep connection, a profound fitness in your being together. If this fitness was based on what you were like when you had lots of time to be together, so much the better. That's the essence of love—that when you manage to come together in a time and place where there's room for warmth and intimacy, you can find it. And if you passed the no-time-for-love test (on page 19) about whether things get better or worse in your relationship when you have a good chunk of time to be together, you know you have this.

If nature intended us to choose our mates based on the weekend marriage, all relationships would begin with a guy who has just started a new job falling in love with a woman who is seven months pregnant. If six months later they're still feeling that they want to be together, then they go forward.

But would they fit together when one day they found they had time for each other? Being great teammates is very different from being great lovers. As it now stands, we start out with lollipops and roses, and if that goes well we make a total commitment to each other and then subject it to our time-starved lifestyle. Maybe there's a deep wisdom in that.

The weekend marriage deprives us of the time we need to have the loving interactions that show we're well matched. You may be great strolling through downtown, commenting on the people you see, stopping to look in store windows, sitting in a Starbucks. But when's the last time you did that?

And you know what happens when too much weekend-marriage time goes by without this? You forget how well suited to each other you are. But now you've been reminded. You do fit well together. And you've seen how to maintain the positive energy that will bring you abundant love in this time-starved world.

PLEASE VISIT ME at *www.WeekendMarriage.com.* We need to share what we've learned with each other about keeping love healthy when we have so little time. It would be great to hear from you.

INDEX

ABOUT THE AUTHOR

With her first two books, Mira Kirshenbaum established herself as an award-winning, internationally bestselling authority on relationships. She has a unique perspective—intensely practical while at the same time generating original research into what works to solve people's problems. *The Weekend Marriage* is her eighth book.

A two-time finalist for the national Books for a Better Life Award, Kirshenbaum is clinical director of The Chestnut Hill Institute in Boston. She has had thirty years' hands-on experience as a leading couples therapist and trainer of therapists. Her face is familiar to people in America and around the world from her appearances on television shows ranging from *The Today Show* to *The O'Reilly Factor*. She was featured in a one-hour prime-time ABC news special.

Showing that she can walk the walk as well as talk the talk, Kirshenbaum is happily married to her college sweetheart. She is the proud parent of two grown daughters.